LORD AMHERST

LORD AMHERST

AND THE BRITISH ADVANCE EASTWARDS TO BURMA

by

ANNE THACKERAY RITCHIE

AND

RICHARDSON EVANS

GYAN

Published by

GYAN

Gyan Publishing House
5, Ansari Road
Daryaganj, New Delhi-110002
Phone: 011-47034999, 9811692060
E-mail: books@gyanbooks.com

Distribution Network
gyanbooks.com
India, USA, Canada, UK, Australia, France

ISBN : 978-81-212-6014-5(PB)
First Published, 1909

2nd Impression 2021

Printed at: Gyan Press, Delhi.

Lord Amherst
Author: Anne Thackeray Ritchie and Richardson Evans

LORD AMHERST

AND THE BRITISH ADVANCE EASTWARDS TO BURMA

BY

ANNE THACKERAY RITCHIE

AND

RICHARDSON EVANS

OXFORD
AT THE CLARENDON PRESS
MCMIX

EARL AMHERST

Aet. 70

CONTENTS

NOTE

The orthography of proper names follows the system adopted by the Indian Government for the *Imperial Gazetteer of India.* That system, while adhering to the popular spelling of very well-known places, such as Punjab, Poona, Deccan, &c., employs in all other cases the vowels with the following uniform sounds :—

a, as in woman : *á*, as in father : *i*, as in kin : *í*, as in intrigue : *o*, as in cold : *u*, as in bull : *ú*, as in rule.

LORD AMHERST

CHAPTER I

FAMILY, EARLY CAREER AND EMBASSY TO CHINA

THE Amherst country lies in that delightful region where the North Downs slope from Sevenoaks to Tunbridge and the Weald of Kent. The place which bears the name is in the parish of Pembury, within a few miles of Tunbridge, and from the Pipe Rolls of 1215 down to the Tudor period we find mention of those who took their description from the spot. The Reverend Jeffery Amherst was, in the time of the Commonwealth, Rector of Horsmonden, a parish east of Pembury, and about eight miles east of Tunbridge Wells. The son, the grandson, and the great grandson of that worthy were successively barristers and benchers of Gray's Inn. The second of these legal dignitaries, who died in 1713, fixed his seat at Riverhead, a pleasant village close to Sevenoaks, and about fifteen miles to the north-east of the original Pembury home. The third of the line of benchers, who also lived at Riverhead, and was buried with his wife at Sevenoaks, was the father of Jeffery, the first Lord Amherst. Another son, William, the father of the statesman whose Indian administration we have here to sketch, was also a soldier.

At Riverhead the Amherst property was close to Knole, and in 1731 the Duke of Dorset procured for Jeffery Amherst, the son of his friend the bencher, an ensigncy in the Guards. This led to service in the Continental wars, and acquaintanceship with the great Captains of the day; and so good a use did the young soldier make of his opportunities, that Pitt recognized in him a heaven-sent agent for work that in the prescient mind of the statesman was of critical importance. It was the period when Montcalm was maturing his plans for connecting the French possessions in Louisiana with the French possessions in Canada. Jeffery Amherst was appointed to the chief command of the operations necessary to defeat this well-laid plan for shouldering the English out of North America. His first exploit was to capture Louisburg, the fortress on Cape Breton which had hitherto mocked the efforts of the British assailants. In the general operations which followed Amherst commanded one of the three forces employed. While Wolfe has obtained unfading renown by the glorious capture of Quebec, Amherst did no less solid service by reducing Ticonderoga. Finally in 1760 the united forces took Montreal, and General Jeffery Amherst was appointed Governor-General of British North America.

In 1761 he was made a Knight of the Bath, in 1763 he returned to England, and in 1776 he was created a Peer. With the rest of his career, his courageous opposition to the wishes of the king, his appointment as Commander-in-Chief, his support of the war with the revolted colonies in America, his action in the Gordon Riots, and his appointment as Field Marshal we have little immediate concern. He went back to live at the family estate at Riverhead, which he called after the scene of his Canadian triumph, Montreal. He was created Lord Amherst with remainder to his nephew in 1788, and died in 1797 at the age of eighty.

We return now to General William Amherst, his brother[1]. He had accompanied Sir Jeffery to Canada, and brought back the news of the capture of Louisburg. Both brothers had a passion for botany, and while in America collected the seeds of many trees and shrubs which were then little known in Great Britain. These were planted in 1759 in the garden at Riverhead in the part which was afterwards known as the American wood. During this time of absence in America, the old house which used to be called Brook's Place was pulled down, and the new mansion finished under the new title. In 1766 Lieutenant-General William Amherst married Elizabeth Patterson. 'She was a very pretty and accomplished woman, much beloved by her brothers-in-law.' William Pitt,

[1] General William Amherst conquered Newfoundland and was for several years Adjutant-General to the Forces.

their eldest son, the subject of this memoir, was born in 1773 at Bath, one of his godfathers being Lord Chatham, who was an intimate friend of the family. Two years after the birth of her daughter, Mrs. Amherst passed away from the love of her kindred. All this while the old Governor-General (Jeffery) was living at Riverhead. General William Amherst had his home at St. John's in the Isle of Wight, where, till his death in 1781, the children lived. The place was then sold, and they went to live at Montreal with their uncle and aunt, who treated them as their own children. The lad went to school at Westminster, and passed thence to Christ Church, Oxford, where he took the degree of M.A. in 1797. In his University days he devoted the long vacations to walking and riding tours, nourishing that taste for scenery and nature of which we shall see so many charming traits in his later life. On leaving Oxford in 1793 he started, after the custom of the time, on a grand continental tour, studying the languages on his way. His capacity as a linguist was shown when, a generation later, an Italian bishop, who found himself in India, spoke of the pleasure he derived from the pure pronunciation with which the Governor-General spoke his native tongue. It was at Rome that in the year 1794 he first met the Earl and Countess of Plymouth, and made great friends of both. After she became a widow he married her in 1800. The marriage, as a perusal of her diary would alone suffice to show, was an exceedingly happy one. She was one of the co-heiresses of the last Lord Archer. She and her sisters were very lovely women.

In 1797, as we have said, the first Lord Amherst died, and his nephew succeeded to the title. He succeeded also to Court favour, and he was Lord of the Bedchamber to George III from 1802 to 1804. His gifts seem to have marked him out very early for diplomatic employment, as in 1809 he was sent as Ambassador Extraordinary to Sicily. In 1815 he was made a Privy Councillor.

From the faithful discharge of these temporary and ceremonial duties Lord Amherst was soon to be called to a mission full of grave political moment and fraught with possibilities of romantic peril. In the early part of the present century the interior of China was still, to the European imagination, a region of mystery, and the Imperial Court was a labyrinth which Western diplomacy had not yet succeeded in exploring. The East India Company, which in India had been transformed from a trading association to a great governing organization, was still on the Chinese coast engaged in conducting and endeavouring to extend a profitable traffic. But the factory at Canton was unauthorized by any explicit warrant from Chinese officials. Nevertheless, in 1813, the Company, anxious to push their trade and influence after the model which had rendered them the leading political power in Hindustán, formally appointed a chief of the factory at Canton. It is a curious illustration of the complexities which the dual system involved, that the Company became embroiled with the local Mandarins less by any act of their own servants than by the independent action of the commander of a king's ship. The immediate result was a series of conferences between high officers of the Company and trusted agents of the Court of Pekin; but it was felt that the differences which existed demanded for their adjustment the despatch of an ambassador extraordinary and plenipotentiary. To this distinguished and trying office Lord Amherst was appointed by the Prince Regent. There had been a British Embassy to Pekin at the close of the preceding century, but the dismissal of Lord Macartney and the humiliating demands made upon him by the etiquette of the Imperial Court furnished no hopeful augury to the new envoy. Lord Amherst, however, started on his voyage with a brave heart and a cheerful readiness to see good in all things. His own account of the long journey from England to the remotest East, as set forth almost from day to day in the diary kept with his own hand, is a record, fascinating in its simplicity, of many strange experiences. Lady Amherst did not accompany her husband on this first excursion to Oriental climes. His son Jeff, whose name appears so often in the faded entries, was the partner of the delights and the privations of this memorable mission.

The narrative of the voyage may serve to remind us of the world-wide domain over which the East India Company in those days had its stations, and left its imprint. The squadron sailed from Portsmouth on February 8, 1816. A visit to Rio de Janeiro, where the British Ambassador had the good fortune to meet the King of Portugal, was a pleasant distraction from the monotony of ship life. A fortnight in the Brazils appears indeed to have been then as common a pleasure by the way as a few days in Cairo is now that the highway to India lies through Egypt. Capetown was then the half-way-house of meetings.

'April 18. In the bay we find the Salsette and five Indiamen homeward bound. I went on board the William Pitt, East Indiaman, to pay a visit to the Countess of Loudoun who is on her way to England. She is going to take her son, Lord Hungerford, to school, and told me that she intended afterwards to rejoin Lord Moira in India. They had had a very tedious passage from Bengal, and had been twelve days in sight of the Cape without being able, from calms and contrary winds, to reach the shore.'

'April 22. Newlands, the country residence of Lord Charles Somerset, as Commander-in-Chief, is in point of situation and external appearance like a gentleman's country house in England. . . . It is pleasantly situated in the midst of flourishing woods, and its neighbourhood affords some most beautiful rides. These are chiefly through an unenclosed country covered with Ericas and various beautiful shrubs. . . . I can compare the country to nothing but a shrubbery suffered to grow wild, and abounding in the choicest and most ornamental plants. . . . One of our rides was, of course, to Constantia, which all strangers visit on account of its famous vineyards.'

On June 9 the party reached Anjier Bay (Batavia), 'exactly the day four months from our leaving Spithead.' Here Lord Amherst could not forbear reflecting on the superior advantages of British rule.

'The English and Dutch system with respect to the natives is as different as possible, for whereas the gates of the fortification are now open at all times, and the Javanese are suffered to wander about the precincts undisturbing and undisturbed, a native under the Dutch Government was infallibly shot at if he ventured to approach the fortification after dark; and I was also told, while taking our walk in the dusk beyond the village, that a Dutchman would not have ventured to have done so as he valued his life.'

After a visit to the city of Batavia he remarks that 'he was greatly disappointed at its general appearance':—

'We rode by the barracks where the Dutch troops used to be quartered, and where it is said the mortality was so great that sometimes two sets of men were swept off in the twelvemonth. The climate appears to have been far less prejudicial both to our civil or military authorities . . . Perhaps the difference in the mortality of the two nations may be owing to the less sedentary and more temperate mode of living practised by the English.'

'In every part of the island'—Lord Amherst observes—'the English travel fearlessly in very small numbers and unarmed, and so far from experiencing injury or insult, have met with nothing but kindness and hospitality.'

Certainly Lord Amherst was an Englishman who believed in England. We had enemies then as now, and their methods in those times were the methods employed to-day.

'The first news the Ambassador received on arriving in Chinese waters was that the Portuguese at Macao had already begun to propagate injurious and unfavourable reports about the mission.'

Upon the fortunes of the Embassy after it had reached Chinese soil, and was subjected to the tender mercies of the functionaries of state, we must not dwell. Celestial diplomacy appears to have been in spirit then what it had been for centuries before and what it remains still. But the contest was waged in 1816 on far different terms from those which the modern Tsung-li-Yamen has to accept. Lord Amherst was necessarily ignorant of the conditions with which he had to deal, and had no means of gauging either the character or rank of the various officials who were successively sent to make experiments on his good nature or his fears. The object was to befool him if possible; if that failed, to terrify him; and if he refused to be coerced, to humiliate him. Throughout the period of cruel indignity and privation to which he was exposed on the very threshold of the palace, he bore himself with rare fortitude and discretion. It is possible that if celestial cunning had not overshot itself by resorting to sheer brutality, the ceremonial obeisance, to secure which all these artifices and outrages had been employed, would have been conceded. For Lord Amherst had it much on his mind to secure for the East India Company at Canton privileges which were dearer in the eyes of Leadenhall Street than the assertion of the dignity of the British crown. There is something at once ludicrous and pathetic in the extraordinary compromises gravely suggested and deliberately discussed on the terrible subject of the Kotow. Reading in Lord Amherst's manuscript the faithfully minute accounts of the trickery by which the Mandarins, without regard to the colour or number of their buttons, sought to entrap him into private and unintended performance of the indispensable obeisance, we can hardly help pitying these artistic rogues at the failure of practices so conscientiously devised and laboriously executed. The end was that the Ambassador had to make a miserable retreat from the outskirts of the Court.

Lord Amherst and his suite were conducted through the inland provinces to Canton. Little by little, as day passed day in the lazy voyage along the Great Canal, vexations and regrets gave way to delighted contemplation of the novel scenes through which he passed. On the whole he had no great reason to complain of want of good-nature in his guides. They allowed him as much liberty as was compatible with their instructions, and the farther he got from the capital the more marked were the attentions paid to him. His reception at Canton was, on the part of the Chinese, so respectful, and on the part of the Englishmen, whether belonging to the factory or the ships of war, so abundantly cordial, that a nature even more resentful and brooding than that of the Ambassador might well have been tempted to forget the injury. But the memory of the affronts he had received could never be effaced. He was delighted with the aspect of the settlement, and was able to solace himself with the thought that the compunction and the fear with which the Chinese authorities regarded their treatment of the Envoy was in itself a pledge that the interests of our enterprise would sustain no prejudice from the diplomatic disappointment. Apart from the official aspect of the matters chronicled, the diary shows Lord Amherst's character in a most pleasing light. Home was constantly in his thoughts. Even the most fantastic scenery on the route suggests to the mind of the wanderer some parallel from the quiet scenes of English towns and fields. Though he does not pose as a naturalist, he took loving note of plants and flowers; and without any pretence to be a connoisseur, he shows a fine appreciation of art in its application to the uses of life. To the charms of landscape he was keenly alive, and of that human nature which his eventful journey presented to him in such bewildering and sometimes repulsive variety, he was a genial student. In everything we see, on the part of Lord Amherst, a high conscientiousness and humble anxiety to support worthily the honour of his country.

The chapter of misfortunes was not ended with the departure from Canton. A visit to Manilla was a pleasant incident in the early part of the homeward voyage, but in passing through the Straits of Jaspar, His Majesty's Ship *Alceste*, which bore the sacred person of the Ambassador, struck on a sunken rock and was lost. Leaving the officers to guard the baggage on the island to which fortunately the whole company were able to scramble, the 'gentlemen' had to take to the boats, and row with infinite toil and discomfort towards Batavia, where, to their relief, they found a hospitable welcome on board an English ship which happened to be in the roads. 'I was overjoyed,' says the patriotic Envoy, 'to find that although the island was given up to the Dutch, the principal English authorities were still at Ryswyck.' The succeeding entries give a suggestive picture of the straits to which a shipwrecked Embassy may be reduced in the humdrum matter of a passage home. At last, all was happily arranged. But when the vessel on which Lord Amherst had again embarked had arrived within 150 miles of the Mauritius, a second calamity ensued in the shape of a fire.

After this there are no more disasters to record.

Stopping at St. Helena, Lord Amherst enjoyed the privilege which sometimes fell to the lot of less distinguished callers at the island. He was admitted to an interview with the captive Napoleon, from whom he heard much that even to-day it is interesting to read. But we can only give the remarks that were personal to Lord Amherst.

'He began by showing me that he had acquainted himself, even minutely, with what related to myself; asked me why I bore the name of Pitt, and if I had not had a *démêlé* with the Queen whom he called an *Intriguante*.'

On August 16, 1817, the much-travelled Envoy had 'once more the satisfaction of setting foot on old England,' and so ends the diary.

CHAPTER II

GOVERNOR-GENERAL OF INDIA

ON January 9, 1823, the Marquess of Hastings quitted the scene of his brilliant labours. It had been a stirring question at home who should succeed the great pro-consul. All eyes were turned to George Canning. He had been President of the Board of Control, but owing to his unwillingness to share with his colleagues the obloquy of the Queen's trial had withdrawn from the Ministry. While he was thus *en disponibilité* news came in the early part of 1822 of Lord Hastings's intended retirement. Mr. Canning needed little persuasion to accept the reversion of a post so attractive to his imagination. No chapter in the volume of 'What might have been's' would be more alluring than that which would deal with the possibilities of English rule in India had George Canning continued the work of Lord Hastings. Possibly he might have discovered, as others have when they pass from the function of control to that of initiative and of executive administration, that the clog is sometimes more powerful in the ordering of events than the driving force. He would certainly have felt with possibly painful distinctness the difference between the system of government in and by a House of Commons moved by fervent speech, and government under conditions where eloquence can only expend itself in the preparation of glowing minutes. But the experiment was not to be tried; the tragic death of the Marquess of Londonderry left a place in the Cabinet to which Canning was imperiously called, and the Court of Directors had to look elsewhere.

Lord William Bentinck had been, some years before, dismissed from the Government of Madras under circumstances which placed him in possession of a well-established grievance. Lord Amherst, on the other hand, was thought to have earned by the hardships he endured in China a title to a reward more substantial than praise. In the case of both the hopes of their friends were ultimately fulfilled, but Lord Amherst's claim was allowed precedence.

There was an interval of more than seven months between the departure of Lord Hastings and the arrival of Lord Amherst. In this brief period Mr. John Adam, who as the senior member of Council was *ad interim* Governor-General, contrived to raise some questions which profoundly stirred the Anglo-Indian community. The freedom of the Press is a doctrine so well established now that it is difficult to enter into the strong convictions of many liberally minded officials seventy years ago as to the necessity of rigid censorship. Lord Hastings had in theory abolished the censorship which indeed had in very rare instances been called into play since the days of Cornwallis. But as after the 'invidious shackles' were broken the editor of a newspaper was still prohibited from publishing 'animadversions on the measures and the proceedings of the Honourable Court of Directors,' and (to omit other forbidden categories) from 'publishing private scandal and personal remarks on individuals tending to excite dissension in society,' the degree of relief cannot be thought extravagant. Mr. James Silk Buckingham, the conductor of a clever little print appearing under the title of *The Calcutta Journal*, for the delectation of society at the Presidency, became the object of a practical demonstration of the meaning of the liberty of the Press. He had ridiculed the appointment of a minister of the Scotch Church to the office of Clerk to the Committee of Stationery. But it must be said, in justice to Mr. Adam's sense of absurdity, that it was the deliberate repetition of the offence which provoked the penalty. Mr. Buckingham was summarily deprived of his licence—for even then a licence was indispensable—to remain in Bengal, and despatched by an early ship to England. It is only fair to those who supported the policy of the high hand to recall the fact that the position of the East India Company as a paramount power was felt, even by those who had played a leading part in advancing the borders of its influence, to be precarious, it may almost be said provisional. The little handful of Europeans at the Presidency represented in the eyes of the native potentates, and the masses of the people, the governing community, and it was plausibly urged that any hesitation on the part of those in authority to assert their title to implicit respect might fatally discredit the exotic administration.

In events of strictly political concern within the limits of India proper, the administration of Lord Amherst was destined to be comparatively sterile. Twenty years before, Lord Lake's campaigns had brought the North-Western Provinces under the Company's rule, and made its officers guardians of the Emperor at Delhi. To Lord Wellesley also we owe the districts which form the Madras Presidency. The main function of Lord Hastings was to reduce to impotence the powers which had long harassed and menaced us in the possession of these territories, but almost all the region which constitutes the Bombay Presidency was incorporated in the Company's dominions as the result of his great campaign against the Maráthás. When Lord Amherst took over charge they had been less than five years under British rule, and five years—even when an Elphinstone is in charge – is hardly long enough to clear away the débris of long confusion. The rest of India east of the Sutlej and the Indus valley was, if we except the territories of Nepál and Burma, &c., in a relation of subsidiary dependence. Throughout Rájputána, Málwá, Gujarát, Oudh, Bundelkhand,

Indore, Bhopál, Berár, Haidarábád, Mysore, and Travancore, the Company spoke through its Residents or other agents with commanding authority.

The disposition of the new Governor-General appeared to mark him out for the rôle of a peace minister. But by the not uncommon paradox of fate the pacific Governor-General had hardly taken the oaths of office when he found himself confronted with the possibilities—soon to become certainties—of hostilities more arduous and more expensive than had been dreamt of in the worst nightmare of the most thriftily-minded magnate at the East India House. The period of Lord Amherst's rule was not barren of domestic incidents, if by the word 'incidents' we may be permitted to describe the stirring of tendencies destined to grow before long into great measures. But his term will be memorable in history for a great war, and a glorious enterprise of arms. The expeditions against Burma marked the renewal, after the repose of thousands of years, of the march of the Aryan eastwards. Many centuries before Christ, the race had poured through the passes of the Hindu Kush into the land of the Five Rivers; had settled in the vast expanse of the Ganges valley, and pushed on wherever the soil was tempting in the highlands and coast tracts of the Deccan. But having thrust aside the peoples of other origin the Aryans appeared content to rest. The mountainous region which divides India from Burma and from China was the limit of their wanderings. Isolated immigrations there might have been of Bráhmans or of Rájputs, but there was no wave of conquest to the east of the Bay of Bengal. Up to the time when Lord Amherst reluctantly accepted the necessity of organizing military measures for the protection of our own soil and the effectual chastisement of Burmese insolence, the basin of the Irawadi was a region beyond the thoughts and almost beyond the knowledge of Anglo-Indian statesmen. We were aware of our neighbours on the west. The progress of Russian arms against Persia, the intrigues which were set on foot, and the combinations which were devised by Napoleon Bonaparte in his palmy days had suggested to the immediate predecessors of Lord Amherst the necessity of cultivating friendly relations with the Court of Teheran[1] and with the great Sikh State on the Indus, which was in the eyes of the diplomatists of the East India Company very much what Afghánistán is at present to the Foreign Office. But with the races and politics beyond our eastern border we had little concern. Missions, indeed, of the most modest character had been sent to Ava with a view to settling

[1] It may be convenient to sum up here Lord Amherst's relations with Asiatic powers on the west by recording that in 1826 Colonel Macdonald was sent as an Envoy to the Shah, who was then vainly resisting an aggressive movement of Russian troops. But the only outcome of the mission was that the British representative looked impotently on while the Czar exacted considerable cessions of territory (Treaty of Turkomanchai, Feb. 23, 1828). The Indian Government helped the Shah to find the money for the indemnity; obtaining, in return for its grant, a release from the obligation to pay a conditional subsidy.

some border troubles, but we had no notion of extending our political activity to the valley of the Irawadi. Yet as the consequence of that first step taken by Lord Amherst, the British standard has been advanced not only beyond the royal cities of the Burmese, but carried up the Irawadi to the very confines of China, and along the tributaries of the great stream, among wild tribes that hardly owned even a nominal allegiance to the lords of the white elephant. This process of undesigned and undesired absorption has added the Celestial Empire to the list of powers with which the rulers of India have to make their account; while it has brought us into perilous contact with the French possessions in Indo-China, and with adventurous soldiers who would fain recover for the arms of the Republic the Empire in the East of which Dupleix dreamt and for which he plotted.

From another point of view the Burmese war marks a stage in the political relations of creeds. Buddhism had its birth in India. From India came the missionaries who won vast populations in Eastern Asia to belief in the teachings of Gautama. But the religion is extinct in the land where its founder was born and where for many centuries after his death it flourished. In the struggle with Bráhmanism the simpler faith of Sakya Muni was worsted, its edifices destroyed, and its votaries exterminated, and so for ages the cults dwelt apart. But when the Hindu Sepoys occupied Rangoon, they found themselves in a Buddhist land. When contemplating the gorgeous pagodas which occasionally served either them or the enemy as fortresses, the Bráhman soldiers might have meditated on the strange fate that again brought the votaries of Siva with hostile intent to the sanctuaries of the milder sage.

The siege of Bhartpur was an episode so stirring and splendid in itself that it seems superfluous to inquire as to its historic significance. If the expeditions against Burma were momentous by their consequences, they cannot be said on the balance of triumph and reverse to have been altogether flattering to British pride. But the storming of Bhartpur, had it been merely a chivalrous blunder, would still have counted for much as a factor in that abiding element of strength—the military prestige of our name. It has, however, a distinct place in the evolution of British power throughout India. It was the brilliant conclusion of the series of arduous labours by which English supremacy had been asserted in Northern India—by which the Maráthá power had been completely crushed, and by which the last faint hope cherished by the puppet emperor at Delhi, or by Rohilla desperadoes, or Rájput princes, or Ját chiefs, was once for all dispelled. The *Pax Britannica* was then definitely extended to the Indus, and though a score of years later the lesson of submission had to be enforced at Gwalior, the victory at Bhartpur may be regarded as establishing the undisputed right of the East India Company to maintain peace and order within the limits of Hindustán and the Deccan.

Chronologically Lord Amherst's administration is singularly well placed for the purpose of comparison. Just half a century had elapsed since the East India Company determined to 'stand forth as Dewan,' and the direct management of the revenue in the districts which then were entrusted to their care passed from the hands of the native officials to those of English 'collectors.' It was about a quarter of a century since the great reforms of Lord Cornwallis placed the administration of Bengal, Behar and Orissa on the basis which has never been abandoned, and which with necessary modifications was adopted for the government of the territories successively occupied as the pillars of the Company's domain were pushed on towards the north and the setting sun. It happens, too, that the term with which we have to do lies almost midway between the installation of Lord Elgin as Viceroy of the Indian Empire of 1893 and the original grant which converted the Company from a trading association into concessionnaires of sovereign rights over a vast tract more populous and more fertile than most European kingdoms. The phases of development coincide, we think, with the divisions into which time has been mapped. It would not be inaccurate to describe the period before Lord Amherst's arrival at Government House, as one of struggle and acquisition, and that which ensued as one of possession and of organization. Vast indeed had been the change in the character of the men by whom the affairs of the people of India were managed, as distinguished from the more conspicuous functions of control vested in the courtiers or the politicians whom the British Cabinet or the Board of Directors sent out to be the agent of their will or—as generally happened, when good work was to be done—to receive instructions which the inexorable course of events had rendered obsolete or mischievous. The Governor-General at Calcutta was a little nearer the realities of the situation than the Commissioners of Control at Whitehall or the Directors at the India House. But closer still to the intrigues of native courts and the humdrum miseries of the seething masses were those illustrious servants of the Company, who, while Viceroys came and went, remained permanently on the field of action, and whose opinions not infrequently dictated decisions to the Governor-General. They possessed the indispensable information, the cultivated instinct, the knack of executive success. Following in their train, and acting loyally in concert with the chiefs in all matters that concerned the *haute politique*, there was already a school of district officials: men whose hearts and souls were absorbed in thought for the well-being of the common folk, who had a mastery of the vernacular speech, and an intimate acquaintance with the infinite variety of native customs and ideas. We would not draw any hard and fast line between the dignified administrator and the magistrate whose highest ambition was to suppress crime, to encourage industry, to enlist all that was best in native society on the side of the new lords of the

State. But it would be irrational and ungrateful, in selecting some names from the roll of honour, to forget the obscure civilians whose fame is confined to the scene of their toil and there is conserved to this day in the traditions of the country side. They had their rewards even in their work. The area of cultivation had not been extended so far as to drive the tiger or game almost as noble beyond reach, and it was still an aphorism with the civilians in Lord Amherst's day that the best work was done when the district officer went amongst the people with his gun on his shoulder. Sport was more than a recreation; it was the means of gaining the confidence of the people and learning the truth about their affairs. The selfish adventurers whose notion of duty was to accumulate a fortune in the shortest time, and hurry back to England to spend it in the purchase of rotten boroughs and huge estates, had ceased to be a recognizable class. The age of the Nabobs had given place to the age of the patriotic, enthusiastic administrators. There were men in high places in Lord Cornwallis's time of singular capacity and perfect integrity; if he had not found such allies he could not have cleansed the Augean stables. But in 1823 devotion and ability had become the rule. The work had trained the workmen.

There were giants in the land when Lord Amherst took his seat at the Calcutta Council Board. The scholarlike Elphinstone; the accomplished Metcalfe; Sir John Malcolm, with his keen and indefatigable temper; Sir Thomas Munro, simple and earnest; Ochterlony—now alas! the shadow of his greater self;—these names are household words even to-day and fill the official literature of the time. Four out of the five were Scotchmen, and three were soldiers. But different social strains were found happily blended in the public service. Metcalfe was a brilliant Eton boy: Elphinstone an aristocrat to the finger tips: Malcolm was a farmer's son: in Munro the plain commercial element was represented. There were strong distinctions of moral and religious tone. We find the gentle spirit of Bishop Heber distressed by tales which he for his part, having known the man, did not believe—that Elphinstone was an 'atheist,' while Munro's letters are full of unpretentious piety. Nor can the student of the times fail to see the contrast between the austere principles of Metcalfe and the somewhat Oriental laxity of Ochterlony. But all had one instinct in common: a commanding sense of public duty.

There was, in truth, giant's work to be done. The Pindárís had been crushed and scattered: the predatory powers brought under the firm bonds of British supremacy. The degenerate descendant of the Great Mughal had to confine his despotic rule to the precincts of the palace or, at most, the boundaries of his private domains. But the submission, though for the moment complete, was sullen, and the only pledge for the continuance of internal peace was the vigilance and sagacity of our officers and the efficiency of our military system. For the former there was abundant guarantee.

> 'The same arts that did gain
> A power, must it maintain.'

But to the adequacy of the Company's armaments, the thrifty spirit of Leadenhall Street was the standing impediment. 'Adapt your revenue to your ruling requirements' was the contention of Sir Charles Metcalfe. 'Adapt your military requirements to the exigences of economical finance' was the unceasing burden of the deputations from home. And in a sense the Directors were right. The disaffection created by excessive or inappropriate imposts is no whit less dangerous than weak battalions, and the problem of finance pressed very heavily on the minds of those responsible.

Revenue means of course for India to a very large extent land settlement. Since the beginning of the century, experience had been secured by our officials at the expense alike of owners and of cultivators. The policy of the Permanent Settlement, which had been adopted for Bengal in 1792 and was subsequently extended to the Benares districts, remained the stock subject of debate in the time of Lord Amherst and remains the stock subject still. With it was conjoined in the talk of officials at Calcutta and Madras or of the district officers as they discussed affairs before the camp-fire in some remote tract, then perhaps first seen by European eyes, the merits of the rival system of Madras. This is not the place to attempt a solution of the insoluble. There is reason in the contention that Lord Cornwallis, by fixing once for all the payments to be made by those who were recognized by him as the landed class, laid a firm basis of loyalty in self-interest. British rule was obviously acceptable to men to whom it assured the easy enjoyment of influence and property. But these eulogists of the Permanent Settlement will not hesitate to admit that, in carrying out the principle, grievous errors were made. The rights of the hereditary cultivators—the true owners of the soil as far as ownership can be said to exist in India—were, if not overlooked, at least left unprovided for, and the right of paying the government revenue, with all the power and privileges that this right implied, was conferred in a great number of instances on men who had hardly any title by long possession and none by prescriptive usage. Even to many of these the headlong gift proved ruinous. The habits of their class had made it morally impossible that they could comply with the stringent conditions imposed as to the payment of the fixed state rent. The result was the wholesale transfer of estates which might well be described as territories to the clever underlings of the English officials. It is a melancholy truth that the first result of our Western administration in the East is to create these opportunities for astute clerks, who have a sufficiently keen intelligence to avail themselves of all the niceties and quibbles of refined bureaucracy, but have not the slightest sympathy with the moral purpose which underlies great administrative schemes. The end of it all was in Bengal that there did grow up a class of men who had a recognized title to what may vaguely be called territorial ownership. In Lord Amherst's time the faults of the Permanent Settlement were more obvious than its merits, nor had the alternative methods adopted in Madras of direct assessments on the proprietary peasants worked to more apparent advantage. Whether the 'village' system was bad *per se*, or worked badly because the assessments were too high, is a disputed matter. It must suffice here to say that the improved ráyatwárí system of Sir Thomas Munro was formally started two years before the coming of Lord Amherst, and that its beneficial operation was one of the noteworthy features of his term of administration.

But the long controversy found a special text in the problem presented by the as yet unsettled tracts of the provinces on the Ganges and the Jumna, and the newly acquired districts which make up the Presidency of Bombay. The best thoughts of some of Lord Amherst's most trusted advisers were given to this—the fundamental issue of Indian administration. Nothing is more pathetic than the tales to which district officers had to listen with impotent regret. There had been violence and confusion in the wild Maráthá days, and from that the conquests and annexations of Lord Wellesley, followed by the brilliant operations of military police carried out by Lord Hastings, had delivered the toiling masses. But in the attempt to grapple with the emergencies of the situation, which the first generation of British officers had to face in the perturbed and harried provinces along the Jumna and the upper course of the Ganges, some of the most tragic blunders of Lower Bengal were repeated. Settlement operations, which are now as familiar to the people as festivals or pilgrimages, were then a bewildering novelty. The initial impulse of the district officer was to frame a register, and unluckily in those prepared in some of the freshly acquired tracts separate columns were allotted to Farmer (in the sense of 'contractor-for-the-payment of Government revenue') and Owner. Our methods of administration had from the first beginnings of the Company's rule been carried out to a great extent through members of the Writer class—a caste of small consideration in native eyes, but indispensable to the working of the exotic method. They have their virtues—industry, pliability, and unquestioning subservience to the express orders and even desires of their superior. But they have their failings also—failings by no means peculiar to the Writer caste,—selfish cunning and rapacity. It was a very simple thing for one of these functionaries, when charged with the preliminary duty of making out the register, to record the owner not as owner but as 'Farmer,' and to avail himself at the earliest opportunity of any technical lapse in satisfying the dues of the State to secure the property for some nominee of his own. A favourite device was to leave the Owner column a blank in the first periodical register (for the settlements were for short terms); in the next to insert a fictitious owner, and in a third to note that it had been transferred by this imaginary person to the clever clerk or his *umbra*. Thus many a family which even in our own day the people regard as the rightful owners of broad lands were transformed into petty tenants, while in a still sadder and larger number of instances the rights dating from the most remote times of village communities were not so much confiscated as ignored. In Lower Bengal, before we had any concern with its government, these ancient Aryan institutions had fallen into decay and had for practical purposes ceased to be. When Lord Wellesley's conquests made the Company lord of new territories on the North-West, the civilians who were despatched to make the first settlements brought with them unfortunately the impressions they had derived from experience in the Lower Provinces. Every schoolboy now knows something about village communities; but it was only slowly that their existence—though they had survived the shock of centuries of change in supreme rule—became apparent to Anglo-Indian officials. It is essential to the due understanding of these initial blunders to remember that after our countrymen had discovered towards the end of the last century the corruption and the incapacity of the native functionaries whom they 'took over' (if we may use the expression) with the grant of the Diwáni, the native element was almost wholly excluded from the administrative hierarchy. Natives were employed as clerks and writers at salaries that were notoriously insufficient to provide them with a decent living. We have seen how they managed to build up enormous fortunes by a dexterous use of the opportunities of their humble state. It was the defect of Lord Cornwallis's system that under it all the ostensibly important and responsible positions were reserved for Englishmen, who had to learn the language and condition, the laws and the usages, of the people as they went on. The number of the foreign officials was, it need not be said, utterly inadequate for the work that lay before them. The reality of power therefore did not correspond with the formal devolution of it. The horde of underlings were masters in all that touched closely the life of the people. Under perfectly regular forms the grossest wrong was done.

It was reserved for Lord William Bentinck to correct this flagrant abuse and to do for the native servants of the Company what Lord Cornwallis had done for the Covenanted Civil Service. But though in Lord Amherst's day there was no definite step towards the creation of an Uncovenanted Service, the need was keenly felt and the reform was ripening in the stage of discussion.

The case was the same with the closely related question of land settlement. Not till 1833 did the cultivating communities of the North-Western Provinces get the Great Charter of their Rights—Regulation IX of 1833. But the district officers had become alive to the real conditions of land tenure and to the magnitude of the injury that had been done. Commissioners had been appointed in 1821 to inquire into all the transfers of property that had taken place during the first decade of our rule in the North-West: and in 1822 the famous Regulation VII was framed, by which at least the sound principle was affirmed. Unluckily the machinery was not provided for the immense operation contemplated, and during Lord Amherst's whole term of rule, in spite of strenuous efforts on the part of the district officers, little advance was made—except, as we have remarked, in the development of opinion. But that was no trifling gain. It was not till 1859 that the tenants, as distinguished from owners, received adequate legal protection. But no reform could make the crooked wholly straight, or efface from the minds of the people the painful recollection of the injuries which British rule in the first instance brought in its train. These, it must be remembered, are the things which make up the history of India for the people of India. The annals of the country are the annals of each district and each village, and no attempt to sketch the events of a Governor-Generalship would be faithful if it did not allude, however superficially, to the cares which oppressed the consciences of those who were in contact with the local realities of life.

The judicial system was hardly less than the question of Revenue Settlements a matter for profound concern. It was indeed forced on the attention of the Calcutta Government by despatches from home. Since 1765 nearly every conceivable method had been tried. Criminal justice had at first been left to native magistrates administering the Muhammadan law. Then the Musalmán code was tempered by English ideas, and the native judges supervised by Europeans. After this, Europeans were set to administer the Musalmán code. Next, the Musalmán code was superseded by the elaborate Regulations of Lord Cornwallis. As a diversion, the Supreme Court, manned by English judges, innocent of all knowledge of India, had claimed jurisdiction over natives and British subjects alike. As to agency, there had been a similar variety of expedients. Magistrates, Collectors of the Revenue, Circuit Judges—these roughly were the three categories to which power was now given, now denied. At one time it was thought a reform to make the collector a judge or a magistrate: at another it was thought a reform to separate the functions. Much the same may be said of civil justice. To grant facilities of appeal was the ideal one year; to limit them was the policy five years after. It was considered a boon to make litigation cheap, until it was discovered that the people would ruin themselves unless it were made dear.

Under Lord Amherst the Cornwallis Regulations were in force, and English judges were the rule.

Revenue functions were kept distinct from judicial. Native jurists were sparingly employed, and only in cases of trifling importance. There was general dissatisfaction. The arrears of work were scandalous: the demoralization of the suitors was a natural consequence. To the honour of the Directors it must be said that in 1824 they wrote urgently recommending the larger employment of native functionaries and of the Pancháyat, or Council of Village Elders, in civil cases. Lord Amherst declared himself heartily in favour of the principle, but urged that as much had been done as could safely be attempted in Bengal. Separate Supreme Courts were established for the North-West — an important step in judicial decentralization. In Madras Sir Thomas Munro had meanwhile taken more courageous steps to train and to employ native judges. Native juries also were made a part of the system; but unfortunately those who were summoned felt it a grievance to have to attend. In Bombay Elphinstone's splendid success in the codification of laws and rules forms a landmark in Anglo-Indian administration. There, too, the more elastic system was adopted and native co-operation enlisted.

The truth is that every great Anglo-Indian, at this time, had his own convictions and preferences as to the proper lines of reform. Some believed in the possibility of reverting to native principles of jurisprudence and of making the Pancháyat—the Court of Elders in the village community — an important adjunct in the administration of justice. Others despaired of restoring efficiency and honesty to institutions which had been demoralized by the long anarchy. Even those who agreed that the judgement-seat must be left to those who held the sword of State, were by no means at one as to the appropriate procedure. The uncertainties and the bewildering bulk of the Regulations were a common matter of complaint. Considering the paucity of capable officials, anything more than a perfunctory compliance with the technical requirements was plainly impossible. The non-regulation system for the newly acquired territories was the happy compromise. This form of administration may be regarded as having first taken definite shape under Lord Amherst. When the Bombay districts first became British, military officers—for want of civilians—were placed at the head of each. Bishop Heber, visiting that Presidency in 1824–5, speaks with enthusiasm of the simplicity and despatch resulting. The principles of the law administered were the same, the application less hampered by form, or by nice distinctions. The plan was adopted subsequently in the Central Provinces—in Tenasserim, in Arakan, in Assam, and has in fact become the normal system for all districts newly brought under our rule. The conventional picture of the Company's servant sitting under a palm-tree, and dealing out patriarchal equity to all comers, was about this time occasionally realized in fact, even in the North-West Provinces. But it was never so common as the picture-books would lead one to suppose. Courts of appeal, whether under the style of Supreme Courts or High Courts, have always been a bugbear to the energetic district official. The lawyers got a footing in the factories of the Company when it was still only a trading association, and ever since have marched steadily in the train of the armies; but seventy years ago there was probably a much closer approach to rough and ready justice than is now possible. The magistrate complied with the formal requirements of the law, but was, it may be suspected, guided in cases of considerable importance to a decision by the hearsay evidence he heard out of doors. Proceedings, it is to be feared, were in this idyllic period often perfunctory, and a great deal of the perjury which is now attributed to the inherent depravity of the average Hindu may be explained by the want of discrimination and care in the old tribunals. It is not that the people believe in lying in the abstract. They have imbibed somehow a notion that lying is the proper thing in an English Court. In this respect the process of amelioration was already beginning in Lord Amherst's time. The necessity of codifying the law was then recognized, though India had still to wait many years for the boon bestowed upon it by Lord Macaulay and Sir James Stephen. There were no doubt gross miscarriages of justice in the somewhat hasty processes of investigation, but if an innocent man sometimes was punished owing to the malice of his neighbours or by want of judgement on the part of the magistrate, the guilty had very much less chance of escape than now. For though the police system was in its infancy the English barrister was almost unknown in the mofussil.

The operations in Burma cost fifteen millions, and as the total revenue for 1822–3 had been little more than twenty-three millions it will be easily understood that the result was grave financial disorder. Lord Hastings had left a surplus of over three millions, and Lord William Bentinck before he resigned restored the equilibrium. But the interim was full of anxiety. The loans by which Lord Amherst met the liabilities of the Government were of course a permanent burden; but it was accounted, politically speaking, an encouraging sign that native bankers were so ready to make advances.

In spite of this grave impediment to progress, it is hardly too much to say that engineering as a branch of State policy began with Lord Amherst. The traveller to-day along the course of the Jumna, when he looks out on a landscape of rich cultivation, does not always remember that the scene as left to us by the native lords was a barren wilderness. Not that the Mughals had been negligent in the matter either of Roads or Irrigation. The works they had constructed remained to remind us of our duty, though in the prevailing anarchy they had become almost useless for want of the necessary repair. Under Lord Minto and Lord Hastings something had been done to make inquiries and surveys. The water of Ali Mardan's canal had once again been brought into Delhi. But it was not till 1823, when Colonel John Colvin—a famous member of a famous corps, the Bengal Engineers—was appointed to be general Superintendent of Irrigation for the Delhi district, that constructive advance began. The Western and Eastern Jumna Canals are the enterprises which chiefly engaged attention in Lord Amherst's day, though they were not completed when he left.

Social reform engaged the attention of Lord Amherst and his advisers. If little in the way of immediate performance ensued, the period was the starting-point of tendencies which, under Lord William Bentinck who succeeded, took precise shape. It was the transition from the epoch of fighting and diplomacy to that of social reform. The arms of the West had triumphed over native prowess, the ideas of the West were now to be brought to bear upon the complex mass of native usage and superstitions. A beginning was to be made with that great policy of education which has brought much of the intelligence of India within the pale of Western culture. Some of the prognostics that may be read in the eloquent letters and minutes of the time have come true. The knowledge of the English language we know now does not necessarily bring with it a grateful or even a candid appreciation of the incidents of English rule, and many of the disciples would perhaps not be unwilling to use the lessons they have learnt for the purpose of superseding the teachers. If the results are not wholly pleasing, let us at least acknowledge that they were clearly foreseen by many who were enthusiastic in promoting the means, and no one who turns from the most insensate ravings of the most disreputable of the vernacular prints of to-day would care to exchange India as we know it with the India depicted for us in the writings of those who knew it seventy years ago.

Of 'Thuggee and Dacoitee' we read much in the correspondence of the period. That strange fraternity which made murder a trade and a cult had found the wild disorder of Maráthá days propitious to their calling, and the formation of robber bands for the sack and plunder of defenceless villages was almost a natural sequel to the overthrow of the predatory powers. The Pindárí, as a Pindárí, found his occupation gone; but when he got back to his village he had still the acquired distaste for ordered industry and the instinct of criminal adventure. Dacoitee indeed is a spontaneous product of the Indian soil, when the powers of supreme husbandry are enfeebled. In addition to the disbanded privates of the robber army, there were also thrown loose upon society their captains, and the swaggering bully with a swarm of armed retainers at his heels was a fairly familiar figure to English travellers. Native territory and the outskirts of native courts were peculiarly their happy hunting-ground.

Nothing is more misleading than the tendency to speak of India as a uniform whole, and we pass gladly from the abuses which lingered round the palaces of moribund dynasties to the utterly wild regions which recent conquest had opened to the civilizing approach of Englishmen. The savagery of the Mers and the Bhíls was proverbial among their Hindu neighbours. Merwárá had been subdued in 1821, and so rapid was the effect of the personal influence of our officers, so little impeded was education by caste ideas, that by 1827 it was found possible to put a stop to female infanticide and to the sale of women. When it is remembered that the former practice was well known to prevail amongst the Rájputs of Northern India, and that long after Lord Amherst's day the most zealous humanitarians confessed their inability to check it—and this in communities of the highest caste—the singular success obtained in dealing with these aboriginal tribes will be appreciated. One of the steps which was most effective in reclaiming the Mers was the formation of a battalion of Mer soldiers. Setting a thief to catch a thief is time-honoured philosophy, and some of the best fighting material of the Indian army is supplied by races whom we should otherwise know as inveterate marauders.

The Bhíls of Khándesh were at first regarded as hopelessly intractable, but much the same method was applied to them as to the Mers, and by 1829 their country, under the admirable rule of Outram, was a model of repose. British rule may be said to have discovered these non-Aryan races which, for want of a better name, we call aboriginal.

Satí was the great moral question of Lord Amherst's time. How familiar the practice was may be judged from the fact that in the year 1819 there were 421 cases in the Calcutta division alone. A *satí* was a popular form of public entertainment, combining a spectacle of devotion in the victim with excitement to the crowd; nor can it be said that in most cases there was any greater compulsion than that of public opinion and the apprehension of social disgrace in case of refusal. There was, however, a very strong body of high official authority in favour of absolute abolition. Opinions had been obtained from pundits which negatived the idea that the burning of a widow on the husband's pyre was an act of imperative religious obligation. We had already ventured to declare the practice of Dhurna criminal, and it was argued that though the prohibition of *satí* might at first cause local trouble, it would in the end be acquiesced in. But Lord Amherst, in opposition probably to the preponderant judgement of his advisers, and certainly to the suggestions of the Directors, refused to incur the political risks of a veto. He trusted rather to the effects of time and growing enlightenment.

The State-system of education may be said to have originated in Lord Amherst's day, but we must dismiss from our minds the notion that either then or for a generation afterwards there was any settled official policy of *popular* education. Colleges and the higher class of schools were alone thought of. The Hindu

College had been opened in Calcutta in 1817, and thanks to the leaven of English culture amongst the native patrons, Western knowledge formed a large element in the training. But on the whole it must be said that the facilities afforded did not attract. In the Benares College rigid orientalism was the rule. Under Lord Amherst colleges were founded at Agra and Delhi; and in many places colleges and schools maintained by missionaries were already giving that sound European education, as to the comparative expediency of which there was doubt and wrangling among the great officials. The controversy, as we know, was decided some years after in favour of Western learning. But the affection of the more learned servants of the Company for the literature and the language, to the study of which they had devoted themselves with so much zeal, is at least intelligible. Yet already the process of anglicization had set in. The Nawáb of Murshidábád amused his leisure with English literature and politics. The King of Oudh patronized European art as well as Oriental philology.

In Calcutta the wealthy natives loved to have their houses decorated with Corinthian pillars, and filled with English furniture. They drove in English carriages with well-groomed horses; many spoke English fluently. In some families the children wore jackets and trowsers. 'In the Bengalí newspapers,' says Bishop Heber, of which there are two or three, 'politics are canvassed, the balance, as I am told, inclining to Whiggism; and one of their leading men gave a great dinner not long since in honour of the Spanish revolution.'

Christian sentiment also was getting into the air; it was the time, we must remember, not only of Henry Martyn and of Marshman, but of Horace Hayman Wilson and of Rám Mohan Rái. If the latter did not quite satisfy the description given of him, that he was essentially a Christian, he represented the movement of rationalizing reform in Hinduism. Protestants and Puritans, Mystics and Rationalists there have been from the first in that vast community, but with Rám Mohan Rái began the phase which has the closest affinities with the thought of the West.

By the 'pious clauses' of the Charter Act of 1813 an English Church establishment had been created for India, that is to say a bishop of Calcutta and three archdeacons were appointed to superintend the chaplains who were already scattered throughout the country as servants of the Company. It is possible to smile now at the earnestness with which this recognition of an English State religion was denounced when it was proposed by Mr. Charles Grant in the House of Commons. Hindus and Musalmáns, instead of rising in protest against this recognition of a foreign faith, were well pleased to see that the new masters were not after all without a creed and a form of worship. Had there been any discontent or ill-will, the journeys which Bishop Heber made throughout British India while Lord Amherst was Governor-

General would have sufficed to reconcile chiefs and people. No official emissary was more welcome at the courts of princes and at the shrines of the idols than the Lord Padre Sáhib, and the journal in which he records his experiences from day to day remains one of the most valuable accounts of contemporary conditions. Not least surely amongst the men who have won great honour for the name of England in India is the gentle and pious Reginald Heber, and his death was one of many sorrows which cast a gloom over the Amherst household.

CHAPTER III

Arrival in India and Social Life at Calcutta

Lord Amherst took with him to India his wife, his son Jeff (whose acquaintance we have already made), and his daughter Sarah. The party started from Southampton on March 15, 1823, in the *Jupiter*, seventy-four guns. Lord Amherst was only just recovering from serious illness, and the early part of the voyage was one of great suffering. His horoscope was certainly not propitious to his fortunes as a traveller, for in an excursion from Funchal a kick from a horse sent the convalescent Governor-General back to his bed. Later they called at Santa Cruz and at Rio de Janeiro—doing ample justice at both places to the marvels and beauty of the tropical scenery. At Rio they found the King of Portugal, and for a second time Lord Amherst made the acquaintance of that singular Court.

On July 18, 1823, they reached Madras, landing in state. Lady Amherst describes the scene :—

'Lord Amherst walked with the members of Government into the Fort; Sarah and I got into a carriage and four, and proceeded to Ameer Baugh, a palace of the Nabob of the Carnatic which he had lent to us. . . . A day was fixed for Lord Amherst to receive the Nabob with much state and ceremony. The potentate arrived with his body-guard, in a splendid low carriage, almost all glass, drawn by four white horses, and accompanied by a brother and an uncle.'

Lord Amherst embraces them all and exchanges courteous civilities by means of an interpreter. The Nawáb was blessed 'with a pleasing countenance and manner,' says Lady Amherst. Lord Amherst having wreathed them with flowers, embraced them again, and took leave, returning the visit next day. Lady Amherst accompanies him, visits the Begums—one of them has been married three years, and is sixteen years old, she has rings on her fingers and rings on her toes, and only goes out in a shut-up box, with a peep-hole to see the country. Lady Amherst is wreathed with flowers and anointed with attar of roses, and before leaving she is treated to a Nautch dance. Festivities of every sort and colour ensue, black and white, with reviews and dinners.

On August 1 the Governor-General and his Lady land at Calcutta; the troops are drawn up, the forts are firing, the river is crowded with vessels, and the shore with spectators. The members of Council receive them at the bottom of the flight of steps at Government House, and conduct Lord Amherst in great state to the Council Chamber where he takes the oath, and a public breakfast in the great marble hall ensued. Lady Amherst holds her first drawing-room on the 17th, which 'was exceedingly splendid' she says, from the number of officers in full uniform, and the large number of troops. 'Surprised we were,' adds the great lady, 'at the well-fashioned dress and manners of most of the ladies.'

Society within the Ditch was in truth large enough and gay enough to distress officials who preferred secretariat delights to social functions. Lady Amherst played a large and gracious part both in court and camp. This lady, who seems to have been a person of great character, courage, and remarkable intelligence, has left a journal, perhaps almost unique of its kind, containing the history vividly and simply told of her husband's rule in India. The past is conjured up, still remembered names are familiarly quoted; we feel the temper of the times.

The events which had so lately shaken Europe had trained a race of warriors. Fighting is the order of the day, danger and adventure are the habitual element in which men live. Wellington has sheathed his sword. Napoleon is safely chained upon his rock, but a whole generation has followed in the steps of its great leaders. India is full of adventures and adventurers. Chieftains and princes have been raised and deposed, the Peshwá's rule has hurried to its close. The campaign in Burma reads like some history from a fairy tale. We witness the march of armies through unexplored lands: amid scenes strangely compounded of splendour and of squalor. We have feats of daring alternating with strange displays of pusillanimity. We marvel now at the cunning of the strange foes—deceptions prolonged till duplicity became almost respectable as an exhibition of ingenuous perseverance in the teeth of failure—now at their dogged courage—now at their fantastic boasts and melodramatic menace. As a part of the stage properties, the golden fetters forged for the Governor-General are particularly effective: but they had a meaning serious enough. There was alarm on the Húglí as well as vapouring on the Irawadi. The narrative has the particular charm of personal feeling. Lord Amherst's keen sense of responsibility would in any case have made him sensitive to every rumour and report; but he had in addition the instincts of a soldier's son. A lover of peace, he was bred in the traditions of the battlefield. His wife shared her husband's anxieties. She had a delicate perception of the picturesque and romantic aspects of war. There are entries that have all the simple seriousness of the comments of a Greek chorus as the action of the piece proceeds. There are intervals of suspense: of eager waiting for news. If only the record covered the whole series of events it might be adopted as the story of the wars. But it would lose something of its charm if it were systematic. We are fortunate in having it as it is, and shall endeavour to weave it into our account of events, and so tinge the matter-of-fact summary with the emotions of the hour.

Lady Amherst had not had the preliminary experience of Asiatic travel which had prepared the

Governor-General for the wonders of Hindustán. She sees everything with clear, but as yet untutored eyes, and we must not, in reading her descriptions, accept in every case her impressions as transcripts of reality. Dainty sketches of figures or buildings enhance the value of the pages; pressed leaves, cuttings from the newspapers of the day, letters received from native friends are laid between.

Before proceeding to the story of Burma and Bhartpur, we may note some passages that illustrate the daily round of Viceregal life. One which bears the date Jan. 5, 1825, at which time Lady Amherst had already sojourned more than a whole year at Fort William, tells of a romantic excursion by river, in the cool morning air, to the ruins of Gaukatchí, which lie just opposite the French settlement at Chandarnagar. Very delightful the ruins must have been, if we may judge from the pen-and-ink sketch of the 'entrance to the Fort'—a fine remnant of the Tudor-Pathan style. Walls and arches are overgrown with saplings and shrouded in palm-trees.

The ladies explore the country round about escorted by the aides-de-camp; and encamp under the shade of forest-trees. The friendly villagers come forward with presents, bananas, oranges, vegetables, 'even jugs of milk,' says Lady Amherst. She gives a pretty description of their progress, she herself riding on an elephant which helps to force the way through the jungle. A vast number of pioneers go in front; cutting through the forest, felling trees covered with fruit and blossom, and making the path possible. The road itself is beautiful and romantically wild. Their train consists of several hundred persons dressed in scarlet and yellow, table-servants, bearers, spearmen, and the crews of the yachts. Lady Amherst and her daughter return home laden, as less exalted ladies might be, with trophies of their excursion, flowers, and plants and sketches.

The following little incident is curious. On April 28, 1825, Lady Amherst and her daughter attend a meeting in the Town Hall to hear a report of the Committee for the native female schools. Mrs. Pearson, Mrs. Shakespear, and Mrs. Harington were present. Lady Amherst says :—

'Mr. M—— got up chiefly to eulogize Mrs. Wilson who manages the schools, after which he launched out into the most vehement abuse of the native religions, several of the principal Baboos being present. It was one of the most ranting and violent discussions I have ever heard. He wound up this strange speech more like a strolling player than anything else, by comparing Mrs. Wilson to Bonaparte and her scheme of education to the road over the Simplon. A clergyman begged leave to propose a vote of thanks to Almighty God for the success of the undertaking. The natives present were evidently much disgusted by this gross impropriety; as to myself and Sarah we were shocked to be made a party to such unwarrantable proceedings.'

Soon after comes a description of a warrior of those days of whom mention will elsewhere be made :—

'Colonel Gardner arrived here from Arakan in a very ill

state of health. He is a very extraordinary man, remarkable for his bravery. He has been in India from his earliest youth, and associated entirely with the natives. He commands a body of irregular horse. . . . Colonel Gardner's own uniform is a high fur cap, short light blue and silver jacket trimmed with fur. His men are dressed like him; they amount to 1,000; and when called upon to face the enemy are entirely to be depended on, would follow him through the greatest dangers and difficulties, and are faithful in all respects when in the field. Out of it, the Colonel says, they would be certain of cheating him. Many years since he married a Begum: his daughter is going to be married to the King of Oudh's nephew. In many respects Colonel Gardner is a native himself.'

On March 12, Lady Amherst describes herself as driving along in Calcutta and meeting a procession, with stands drawn by men and bullocks, with bands of native music, and harlequins and tomtoms:—

'One special company of natives was screaming with laughter, and in the midst of them a man, dressed like one of our Methodist preachers, addressing the multitude. The magistrates hearing of it, the man was taken into custody and fined for turning the Christian religion into ridicule. The Methodists are specially obnoxious to the natives, their familiar style disgusts them, and entirely counteracts their avowed system of conversion. The above festival was in honour of a rich Baboo.'

Among the many amusing facts which relieve the gloom of the news from Rangoon, is the account of the native lady at Calcutta, who shammed ill, and whose anxious husband, a rich Babu, called in the Governor-General's doctor. The lady, who had played this prank to beguile the dreary hours of the zenana, burst out into fits of uncontrollable laughter when the doctor was introduced. The doctor seems to have been greatly fascinated, and describes her as a very beautiful girl of seventeen or eighteen years old, with the most perfect symmetry of features he had ever beheld. He left her perfectly well; as he came away he observed multitudes of young females at all the doors and windows tittering and laughing too.

We are still in 1825. June has come with its torturing heat. Lord Amherst had still to discover Simla for the comfort of his successors: and the Governor-General's lady, like other wives of Anglo-Indians, had to make the best of existence in the plains. She thus describes a health excursion up the river in the Government yacht, the *Soonamookie*:—

> 'Our party was small, consisting only of Lord Amherst and myself, Sarah and Jeff, Captain Dalgairns, Captain Crole, Mr. Hale, Mr. Marriage, and Dr. and Mrs. Abel, in all ten persons. Pinnaces, budgerows, paunchways, and baggage boats to the number of about fifty; and the servants, boatmen, guard of Sepoys (the latter about forty), in all, amounted to about 500 men.'

They sailed on past the junction of the Húglí with two other rivers by Nadiyá—then described as looking 'nothing more than a native village of huts.' On the 29th they anchored. Lady Amherst describes indigo plantations, palm-trees, and bananas, herds of cattle, tumble-down villages haunted by crocodiles, and the thunder and lightning at intervals. The thermometer is ninety-two, but the air is fresh. They start in the early mornings, sailing between beautiful banks, passing native towns and villages, curious temples and buildings, and are once driven aground in a storm. Then they come to the ever famous plains of Plassey. In the evening the ladies go on shore for a walk by the indigo plantations, they collect a few insects and plants, but it is soon too dark to go further. On July 3, 1825, they are still proceeding on their way to Murshidábád, and the Nawáb of Bengal sends them boats full of fruit and flowers, as do the Resident and Agent at Murshidábád. On the 4th they anchor at Berhámpur, and greatly admire the place and the buildings among the groves. A few miles further on they enter the town of Murshidábád, full of beautiful buildings with fine trees upon the banks. It seemed to be composed of native huts. There were, however, some large handsome buildings belonging to the Babus, and an immense number of Hindu temples of various forms, most of them extremely beautiful; the dome of one of these was ornamented with numerous conical small domes, which had a rich and new effect. The Rájá of Bengal has a large house upon the banks, he is a child of nine years old under protection of the Government, he is already crowned, and is about to be affianced to his cousin.

On July 7, 1825, they are still sailing agreeably on the river, and they meet a large herd of bullocks swimming across the stream, their drivers swimming after and guiding them. 'On the 8th and 9th the heavy rains begin, thermometer eighty-two, the river enormously wide' writes Lady Amherst. Fresh and new as the sights are to the travellers, it seems needless to recapitulate the items of temples, villages, and mango groves by which they pass, and which Lady Amherst enumerates. Sometimes they land, to the surprise of the villagers, and take walks upon the banks. They are exposed to some danger from the sudden storms which now begin to overtake them on their way. It is not until the 20th that they arrive at Barrackpur on their return journey to Calcutta.

In August, 1825, Lady Amherst had an attack of cholera. She is evidently a person of admirable nerve. She makes little of her own illness and goes on keeping her diary notwithstanding. On the 18th she writes:—

'This dreadful scourge still rages at Calcutta, and its environs, and Barrackpur. Dead bodies lie in heaps by the river-side. At Achipur the same disease extends, notwithstanding a grand sacrifice by the Hindus of a live buffalo, a goat, and a dog.'

It was certainly a melancholy season. As the result of the cholera Lady Amherst records the *satís* close to Calcutta and the 'murders,' as she says,

'One can give no other appellation. Along the river the poor creatures are brought screaming that they are not dying, but the Bráhmans are inflexible and suffocate them with mud.'

There is a pleasing account of a Burmese princess,

the Ránì of Cheduba, who, having been made a prisoner with her husband in one of the early operations of the Burmese war, was detained in honourable captivity at Calcutta :—

'Living in Fort William in a neat pretty house within the walls, she has liberty to walk about and do as she pleases. She has declined a house in Chouranghee, which has been offered to her. She has written me a letter in the Burmese language and character, in reply to some inquiries I made after her when a child in the family died. She has sent me two pocket-handkerchiefs worked by herself, and most beautifully and curiously, in the style of lace, which she wove with her fingers without any other implement. She is the most industrious little woman possible, always either reading, writing, or at work; never for a moment idle.'

The letter, which has a strange cabalistic appearance, is preserved among the English lady's notes.

We may as well finish here by anticipation the story of this interesting captive. The conclusion of peace with Burma brought her an unwelcome release. On June 9, 1826, Lady Amherst takes leave of her.

'She is very much grieved at quitting Calcutta and us; we have seen her frequently; her affectionate disposition has attached us all much to her; she appears very apprehensive as to her reception by the king and queen of Ava, and frequently expressed the fear that she would lose her head. . . . The Rájá, her husband, is quite a brute; she showed us wounds and scars inflicted by him.'

The last news we get of her is in a letter from Rangoon, in the August following. Mr. Crawfurd gives an account of the poor lady, who was evidently regretting her lodgings in Fort William, and very uneasy as to her fate.

This second volume of the diary concludes with an account of Bájí Ráo, the famous Peshwá,

'who in the last Maráthá war caused so much fatigue in pursuit, and hard fighting to the British troops, under Lord Hastings. Captain Low[1] has had the custody of him ever since, and says he is one of the best mannered Indians he ever saw. His conversation is superior, gentle, and temperate. His mad ambition has softened down into luxury, ease, and idleness; and the worship and rites of his gods at present is his only occupation. The enormous allowance of eight lacs of rupees, paid by the Company to him ever since he was taken prisoner, and the Maráthá power destroyed, enables him, his family, and followers who are very numerous, to enjoy every kind of luxury.'

We are now in October, 1825, and the beginning of the cold weather. A ghastly event has just occurred in the immediate neighbourhood of Calcutta:

'A young man having died of cholera, his widow resolved to mount the funeral pile. The usual preparations were made, and the licence procured from the magistrate. The fire was lighted by the nearest relations; when the flame reached her, however, she lost courage, and amid a volume of smoke, and the deafening screams of the mob, tomtoms, drums, &c. she contrived to slip down unperceived, and gained a neighbouring

[1] Familiar to so many as Sir John Low, K.C.B., of Chatto, in Fife. My father has told me that in those early days he was offered a lac of rupees on one occasion, only to allow one elephant to precede another in some public procession.—A. T. R.

jungle. At first she was not missed, but when the smoke subsided it was discovered she was not on the pile, the mob became furious, and ran into the jungle to look for the unfortunate young creature, dragged her down to the river, put her into a dingy, and shoved off to the middle of the stream where they forced her violently overboard, and she sunk to rise no more.'

'It is a miserable reflection,' says the writer, and indeed one can well imagine what the horror of such events must have been happening within a few hundred yards of home. At any time of public mortality these sacrifices rise enormously in numbers.

All through the diary these miserable histories alternate with episodes like chapters out of the *Arabian Nights*. Here, for instance, is the visit of Ráj Garoo (illustrated with a clever sketch in pen and ink). He is supposed to be a priest of eminent sanctity, and enormous wealth, and appears with a long suite of attendants. On entering the Audience Chamber and being presented to the Governor-General he did not bow or make any obeisance, but a slight motion of both hands which meant his blessing.

'We were all surprised to see so good-looking and young a man, who appeared under thirty-five, with a very benevolent smile and a dignified manner. He said in Persian that his first pleasure and duty in life was to pay his adorations to Jagannáth, which he was on his road to do, and the next object, which was both a duty and a pleasure, was to pay his respects to the Governor-General, who accordingly returned a courteous answer. After some complimentary conversations Lord Amherst put a long string of pearls round his visitor's neck, and the young priest offered some very handsome presents of shawls and gold and silver muslins, very beautifully worked; also pearls, coral, and gold and silver tissue; these were placed on carpets and silver waiters on the floor of Lord Amherst's ante-room. As presents are not allowed to be accepted, we selected a few to purchase. The Gaussein (Holy Man) now rose, and expressing in elegant language the satisfaction he had felt at the interview, withdrew. We were all charmed by his manners; his dress was simple, a plain muslin vest down to the wrists, and crossing before with a good deal of drapery of the same material round his waist, in the curl of each ear two of the very finest pearls I had ever beheld.'

It appears later on that this holy priest was a spy making his own observations on behalf of the Burmese Court, as he paid his devotions by the way to Jagannáth and the Governor-General of India.

CHAPTER IV

THE BURMESE WAR: THE CAPTURE OF RANGOON

ALMOST from the moment when Lord Amherst addressed himself to the duties of his high office, the contingency of war with Burma occupied his thoughts. The occupation of Bengal had brought the authority of the Calcutta Government into contact at many far distant points with the huge empire over which the successors of Alompra either held sway or claimed sovereignty. Far away to the north the officers of the Company in what was then the outlandish district of Rangpur looked across with curiosity rather than with covetousness to the great valley of Assam. More to the south the British district of Sylhet marched with Cachar. On the seaboard of the Bay of Bengal, Chittagong was our farthest outpost, from which stretched southward along the coast what was once the famous kingdom of Arakan. But all the regions we have named, though for our present purpose they must be treated as held or claimed by the Burmese, were in truth mere outlying and detached fragments of the vast kingdom which was ruled from Ava. Assam is the upper portion of the basin of the Brahmaputra, which flows into the Bay of Bengal. Burma, including in that term the lower province of Pegu, consists roughly of the valley of the Irawadi, which flows into the Gulf of Martaban. The watershed which divides the two is a vast expanse of mountains peopled by wild tribes, barren, inhospitable, and all but impenetrable. A huge spur, projecting from this central mass towards the west, divides Assam from Cachar. The main mountain system continues southwards in a direction roughly parallel to the coast, thus dividing the comparatively level strip of seaboard, called Arakan, from the basin of the Irawadi, that is to say from Burma and Pegu. Thus the land barrier is practically complete from the gigantic mountain masses of the Chinese frontier to Cape Negrais on the south, where the coast suddenly turns to the east and forms, beyond the rib of hills, the Delta of the Irawadi.

But even now we have not completed our survey of the theatre of the coming war. Beyond the limits of Pegu, and separated from it by another system of hills, lies the valley of the Salwín, and from the mouth of this river, which is hardly inferior to the mighty Irawadi, stretches still southward much in the same way as Arakan the coast territory of Tenasserim. We have described the interior of Burma as ground almost untraversed by European feet, but centuries before the coast had been the haunt of Portuguese adventurers, whose exploits and whose crimes form one of the most fascinating chapters in historical romance. But these men were pirates or bandits, renegade priests from Goa, or deserters from Malacca. Like others of their nation, they showed a marvellous capacity for adapting themselves to native ways and surpassed Asiatics in the favourite forms of Asiatic crime. Their descendants remain to this day by thousands in the East, and are hardly distinguishable in morals or physique from the indigenous natives. Pirate ships from the Portuguese headquarters in the Sundarbans swept the seas; one clever miscreant set up a kingdom for himself at Syriam near Rangoon, and kept up gorgeous Oriental state. But practically the struggles for mastery in Burma were amongst the natives whose only relations with Western arts and civilization arose from the occasional employment of mercenary Portuguese captains.

We need not dwell upon the monotonous and sanguinary record, or chronicle the ups and downs of fortune by which the kings of Burma conquered the kings of Martaban or of Pegu, or these States in turn obtained control over the northern kingdom or each other. It is however worth while to note that Siam entered constantly into the competitions and complications just as in our own day a definite understanding with the Court of Bangkok was regarded as a necessary factor for the success of administration at Mandalay. It suffices to go back to 1750, when Alompra[1] the Hunter, a man of humble birth but commanding

[1] Alaung-payá.

genius, displayed a spirit of sincerely national patriotism which is rare in Oriental annals, and established for himself and his descendants a throne on a firm basis at Ava. By this time some European factories had been founded on the coast. It was a circumstance of evil omen that the servants of the East India Company, who had their quarters in the Island of Negrais, helped Alompra's rival in Pegu by the sale of munitions of war, and paid with their lives for their double dealing. If strength of character be a merit, Alompra is entitled to his renown. But his successors imitated him rather in his pride than in his faculty for command, until Thebau, the feeblest and the last, passed from the scene of his misrule, and all Burma became a British Province.

It is customary to speak of the Court of Ava, but in truth the capital has been changed from time to time according to the caprice of the reigning sovereign. The magnificent ruins of pagodas and palaces remain at many places on the banks of the Irawadi to remind the passing voyager of the mutations of Royal state. Pagan and Ava and Amarápura have had their day and ceased to be. It must at least be allowed that the house of Alompra gave their subjects an imposing show of kingly state and impressed their imagination by the most unsparing acts of despotism. They might have remained undisturbed to take their chance of native rivalry if they had been content to allow the English to rest in peace within the confines of India.

But before the beginning of the present century

troubles arose. The Burmese monarch of the day had sent an army through a defile of the mountain barrier, had conquered Arakan and extinguished the glories of that ancient kingdom. To make intelligible what would otherwise appear to be the prepcsterous claims advanced a quarter of a century later, it is necessary to remember that the authority of the Arakanese monarchy, while it flourished, had extended as far as Dacca, so that a precedent could be cited for the pretensions of the Burmese sovereign to exercise lordship in Bengal.

But Arakan did not accept the rule of the stranger with docility. A sentiment that deserves to be called national animated the bulk of the people, and the oppression of the Governor to whom the management of the province was entrusted converted ill-will into active disaffection. The Náf estuary was the boundary between Arakan and the British district of Chittagong, and over it passed band after band of emigrants from the south. Some of these established themselves in the wild tracts near the frontier and thence made incursions into the land that had been their home. It may be assumed that the Burmese had a perfectly genuine contempt for the resources of the East India Company, but when the leader of a Burmese force came into British territory in pursuit of a band of these marauders he preferred a comparatively modest claim for the surrender of the fugitives. Still to leave no doubt of the firmness of his determination he established himself in a stockaded camp. Sir John Shore was not easily moved to anger, but he felt unable to tolerate this violation of our territorial rights. By a sufficiently transparent compromise it was arranged that if the Burmese withdrew, the Company would surrender the fugitives. This was done, doubtless on high moral grounds, but with considerable injury to our prestige, nor did the despatch of Captain Symes on 'a friendly mission' to Ava tend to correct the impression.

The result was precisely what might have been predicted, there were further emigrations of fugitives into Chittagong, and further pursuits by armed Burmese forces. An attempt to dislodge them was repulsed, but Lord Wellesley had his hands too full of wars elsewhere to be able to take serious note either of the insult or of the reverse. The conscience of the Company, moreover, was not wholly clear; with a view to putting British authority in the right, arrangements were made for settling the fugitives in large industrial communities. When the Governor of Arakan still pressed his demands, Lord Wellesley resorted to a diplomatic subterfuge and affected to assume that it was the unauthorized indiscretion of a local functionary. Again Captain (by this time, Colonel) Symes was sent to Ava, but hardly succeeded in obtaining a courteous hearing from the king. It is easier, it must in candour be said, to state the issues than to pronounce final judgement on the equities of the dispute. On the one side was the piteous plea of the fugitives, 'We will never return to the Arakan country; if you choose to slaughter us here, we are ready to die; if you drive us away, we will go and dwell in the jungles of the great mountains.' On the other, was the case of the king, 'If you keep in your country my slaves, the broad path of intercourse between the states will be blocked up.'

In the year 1811 the question had become a burning one, and for a time the rights and wrongs of the 'Mugs' was a topic of interest to sentimental politicians even in England. This cacophonous name was given indiscriminately to all the Arakanese, though in strictness it applies only to one section of the population, said to be descended from Bengalí mothers and Arakanese fathers. Amongst the suffering race appeared in 1811 one who for a time seemed destined to be the saviour of his country. Khyen-byan, whom the Anglo-Indians persisted in calling King-bering, was the son of the district officer who had betrayed Arakan to the Burmese. So unpopular was he on this account amongst his countrymen that their hatred followed the son to his exile in Chittagong. But he was soon to free himself from obloquy. Half brigand, half patriot, he collected a host with which he invaded Arakan, captured the chief town, and behaved with the usual licence of a Burmese victor. Again the Governor of Arakan held the English responsible, and again Calcutta statesmanship professed its innocence. This time Captain Canning, who had twice before visited Rangoon on diplomatic business, was despatched to Amarápura, to smooth away the displeasure of the king. But so little did he succeed in mollifying the angry feelings of the Court, that it was only by address and determination that he escaped being detained as a hostage. This was the last attempt to communicate with the government of Ava by a pacific British mission.

The nationalist drama, in which King-bering was the leading actor, had an ill ending. A Burmese army came and swept him and his followers back to Chittagong, from which harbour of refuge they resumed patriotic incursions. So, till 1815, the triangular warfare was maintained, poor King-bering and his men being hunted with equal zest by the Company's Sepoys and the levies of the Viceroy of Arakan. Then the freebooter died, and his haunt amid the forests knew him no more. But the ill-feeling, of which his forays were the occasion, did not die with him. It would be too much to say that King Bodau Phra[1] brooded over his wrongs; but the inattention of John Company to his representations struck him as a piece of outer barbarism, of which the government of Ava was obliged to take serious note. It was intimated in 1817 that if the vagabond Mugs were not sent back to receive the penalty of their contempt, the Lord of the Seas and Earth would be obliged to re-assert his authority over such places as Dacca and Murshidábád—undoubted appanages of the crown of Arakan. Such was the warning, given in a pompous letter from the Governor

[1] Bodaw-payá.

of Arakan—the Rájá of Ramrí. It came into bad hands, for the Marquess of Hastings was now supreme at Calcutta. The statesman who found means to dethrone the Peshwá was not disposed to yield to the menace of 'The Golden Foot.' The answer was a simple statement that the British could not and would not deliver up those who had sought and had, some of them for thirty years, enjoyed their protection. Perhaps the news of recent events in Central India co-operated in persuading the king not to commit himself to open hostilities. At any rate he died, in 1819, in peace, his dignity unimpaired, and his realm at the height of its greatness.

It was in quite another direction that his successor prepared to enlarge the bounds of his dominion. We have no intention of attempting to elucidate the politics of Assam. It is enough to say that this secluded kingdom enjoyed the blessings of a peculiarly limited monarchy. There was a Rájá and a council of three ministers. The monarch could do nothing—not even get himself crowned—without the permission of his advisers; but he was able to dismiss any of them in favour of some more agreeable member of the same family. While this was the judicious balance of power in the highest place, the real functions of administration were fulfilled by provincial officers, nominally subordinate. The arrangement, which we believe had long prescription in its favour, broke down in 1809; and the end of an extremely complicated system of court intrigues was the entry of a Burmese army and the deposition of the king. A kinsman took his place, and piously contented himself with slitting the ear of the fallen 'King of Heaven.' After a time of exile in Bhután, the dethroned king ventured back, and for a while recovered power. The Burmese, however, proved treacherous allies, and again the poor king had to fly; but on this occasion he found refuge in the adjacent British district. Thus the Company had a Shan pretender on its hands in Rangpur as well as a community of fugitive Mugs in Chittagong. History repeated itself. The commander of the Burmese forces in Assam threatened to pursue the royal refugee; the Company's 'Commissioner of the North-East Frontier' prepared to repel aggression.

We have now to turn to the third—and, happily, the last—point at which, on the eve of Lord Amherst's administration, the Company had strained relations with the representatives of the Court of Ava. The ancient valley kingdom of Manipur hardly calls for any detailed description. The tragic massacre of an English Envoy, of which it was the scene only a few years ago, made its position, its characteristics, and even its physical aspect, familiar to the most phlegmatic of home-keeping Britons. It will be remembered that of the columns which were despatched to restore order and exact reparation, one advanced by way of Cachar and another by way of Upper Burma. This fact supplies the key to the events of 1823. So far back as 1762 a treaty of alliance had been concluded between the Rájá of Manipur and the English Governor of Fort William in Bengal. A small force of Sepoys was even sent with the object of helping the Rájá to expel the Burmese who were then, after strange vicissitudes of conquest, in occupation. The attempt was abandoned. Passing over more than a half century we find the Burmese advancing into Cachar, with the intention of dealing with certain Manipuri princes who, driven out of their own country, had taken up their quarters there. But they had been anticipated by the extension to the region of British protection. Again the demand for the surrender of fugitives was preferred, and again it was met with a decisive refusal; and so, when the year 1823 closed, a Burmese host was hanging menacingly on the Sylhet frontier.

The three tracts, which were soon to be the scene of hostilities, are now among the most valuable of our Indian possessions. The tea-gardens of Assam have attracted from other parts of the continent a coolie emigration so considerable that the control of it is a most important feature in executive action, while the growth of trade at Akyab on the Arakanese coast is one of the stock marvels of industrial annals. But, in 1823, cultivation was the exception, and commerce was of the most primitive description. We have still, from time to time, to send a force into the hills to chastise one of the tribes, Abors or Lusháis or Nágás, who descend from their mountain retreats to raid upon the peaceful settlers in the valley. The obstacles which beset these expeditions when they have passed from the jurisdiction of the English magistrate into the hilly wilds is a measure—though an imperfect measure—of the conditions with which the leaders of our first advance had to contend, while they were still in the cultivable but neglected lowlands. The gigantic system of navigable rivers in India did, to some extent, facilitate the transport from the Presidencies to the distant frontiers—even in the days before railways had revolutionized the art of campaigning. But the absence of roads and bridges was the grave impediment.

On January 17, 1824, the first serious collision took place. A body of 4,000 Burmese and Assamese had crossed the mountains from Assam and takon up an entrenched position at Bikrampur, a plàce forty-five miles east of Sylhet, while another force, flushed with victory over native foes, was advancing from Manipur. To prevent the junction of these two, a detachment of Sepoys and local levies, which had been posted to observe events a little beyond our frontier, marched to the attack of the Burmese entrenchments at Bikrampur. The enemy were put to flight, but managed to join the host from Manipur. Some further successes were obtained by the Company's troops, but a gallant attack made on the stockade constructed by the Burmese on the Surmá failed. Since 1824 we have had wars in so many quarters of the globe that hardly any fresh modification remains to be discovered. The 'laager,' the 'zareeba' have become household words. But the first experience of the stockade was a discouraging surprise.

The effect of our repulse was further to inflate the pride of the courtiers of the Golden Foot. They were under the same delusion as those who, in 1857, were responsible for the worst horrors of the Indian mutiny. The English, it was supposed, were a mere handful of traders, hiring Sepoys to do their fighting, but possessing no reserve of military strength.

The British reverse in Cachar occurred in February, 1824. On the 24th of that month the Declaration of War was published in Calcutta. The immediate provocation came from the Chittagong borderland. At the mouth of the River Náf lies the small island of Sháhpuri. Here had been established a military guard with a view to putting a stop to the incessant molestations of which British subjects were the victims. Tolls had been levied by Burmese officials on boats passing to and from Chittagong. In one instance, when payment was refused, shots were fired and one of the crew killed. The whole attitude of the Burmese was wantonly aggressive. Seizures of persons working on British soil were frequent. There were great gatherings of armed men on the Arakanese side. The king's officers affected to take umbrage at our calling the island ours, and they sent a large force which very soon expelled the little garrison. This manifestly could not be endured. A strong body of regulars was despatched from Calcutta to reoccupy the post, but before it arrived the Burmese had the discretion to retire. The Governor-General had expressed his willingness to appoint Commissioners to determine the question of ownership; an offer which was only interpreted at Amarápura as a proof of conscious weakness. Lord Amherst, however, who was still painfully anxious not to be led astray like his predecessor, and to abide by the pacific instructions of the Directors, was careful to keep the door of reconciliation open. Even in the Declaration of War he 'retained an unfeigned desire to avail himself of any proper opening which may arise for an accommodation of differences with the king of Ava.' But he made 'the tender of an adequate apology, and the assurance of such terms as are indispensable to the future security and tranquillity of the Eastern frontier' a condition. As well might Jack the Giant Killer have sent up a conciliatory message when he knocked at the door of the Giant's Castle. The Viceroy of Pegu, who had acted previously as the mouthpiece of the Court, replied. He claimed Dacca and Chittagong for his master; asserted that Sháhpuri was indisputably Burmese, and graciously recommended the presumptuous person at Calcutta to say whatever he had to say by way of petition to Maha Bandúla.

The die was cast. The Company was at war again, and the operations promised to be of a more than usually expensive kind. Lord Amherst—still new to the ways of administration—had to face the responsibilities of conducting a peculiarly difficult campaign.

We have remarked already on the strange apathy that had been shown by earlier Viceroys as to collecting accurate information about Burma from the traders, residents, and missionaries who might at least have given useful hints. Lord Amherst had to rely almost wholly on the report of Captain Canning, and as the lines on which operations were subsequently conducted were unfavourably judged by some contemporary critics, it may be as well to give a condensed extract from the document.

'Should an advance to Amarápura be contemplated, a larger force of 3,000 Europeans and 7,000 natives would be necessary. This, with a proportional detail of artillery and particularly gun-boats, would place the capital in our possession.

'Rangoon is accessible at all seasons, but during the strong prevalence of the south-west monsoon, from the beginning of July to the end of September, there is risk. . . . For the advance of a force on the capital the commencement of the rains or the beginning of June should be selected, and the rise in the river removes all obstacles from sand banks, &c., and a strong southerly wind would convey the troops to their destination in a month or five weeks.'

Captain Canning cannot make even a distant conjecture as to the number of men the Burmese could bring into the field. The absence of data is well illustrated by the fact that the population is variously estimated at from three to eighteen millions.

'Of a regular army they have no idea. When troops are required, each district of a province is assessed at a certain number of men. . . . The men thus raised receive no pay; in lieu of which they are provided with food. Powder and ball each man manufactures from the raw materials supplied him by the Government. . . . At close quarters the dah, a species of broadsword, is in the hands of the Burmese a formidable weapon. Strength and individual courage they possess in a high degree.'

It would thus appear that according to the best expert advice procurable it was advisable to take Rangoon—if it was to be taken at all—by a sudden *coup de main*, and that the ascent of the river to Amarápura would be easy. If the latter prognostic was not fulfilled, the explanation is the unlooked-for subtlety of the Burmese tactics. Yet Captain Canning estimated their defensive power more highly than Sir Thomas Munro, who was at the time of all Indian statesmen and soldiers the most competent to form a sound judgement.

A letter addressed by Lord Amherst on March 10 to the sagacious and experienced Governor of Madras is interesting in two ways. It shows that Lord Amherst was not carried away by the sanguine views of those around him; and that he did not base his plans on the assumption that there would be a river promenade to the capital. It exhibits also in a most pleasing light the modesty and courtesy which Lord Amherst carried into all official relations.

'Captain Canning will be directed, on our occupying Rangoon, to tender from thence to the Burmese Government the terms on which we shall consent to make peace. Meanwhile, every possible inquiry will be instituted at Rangoon into the practicability of procuring a sufficient number of boats to transport an army of eight or nine thousand men to Amarápura.

'I should hope that though the main enterprise may be relinquished, the possession of Rangoon, Cheduba, and perhaps other ports or islands belonging to the Burmese, may induce them to accede to such terms of peace as we shall propose.

'It is really with considerable hesitation that I have entered into this detail with you. Arrangements like these are far beyond the reach of my experience; and I may have overlooked objections which would readily present themselves to persons more conversant with these matters.'

One other set of passages from a letter of April 2, 1824, may serve still further to illustrate Lord Amherst's ideas for the campaign.

'The aid to be derived from the Siamese, in the event of protracted hostilities, has entered deeply into our calculation. But I am not disposed, if we can possibly avoid it, to engage too largely in the intrigues and politics of the Indo-Chinese nations, or to enter into engagements which we are not prepared at all hazards to fulfil. Our main object will be, not the acquisition of new territory, but the security of that which we already possess.... The only tribe to which we have yet held out hopes of independence is the Assamese. These were annexed about four years ago to the kingdom of Ava, and it is highly desirable on every account that they should no longer remain subject to the Burmese yoke.'

There were of course other modes of approach to Amarápura. Burmese hosts had passed through the wilderness of mountains to Assam and to Arakan. Why should not a small well-equipped force of

Sepoys and Europeans use the same route? The answer was that a tumultuous levy of natives who can live on almost nothing, who can plunder or carry the little food they need, who can dispense with shelter, who know the country thoroughly and are accustomed to the climate, and whose individual lives are in the esteem of their commander valueless, could do what a costly disciplined column under European guidance would perish in attempting.

There was a special reason for the call made upon Sir Thomas Munro's good offices. The Bengal army was recruited in the main from the higher castes, and viewed with religious repugnance the notion of crossing the 'Black Water.' As it would have been out of the question to reach Rangoon save by sea transport, recourse was had to the less scrupulous material presented by the Madras army. Happily Sir Thomas Munro was as popular as he was capable: and the response to the appeal from Calcutta was immediate and enthusiastic. Colonel M'Creagh led the Bengal division, Colonel Macbean was at the head of the more important force supplied by Madras. Sir Archibald Campbell was in supreme command. Altogether the army of the Irawadi comprised over 11,000 men. Of these one half were Europeans, one of the regiments being the Madras European regiment. The voyage was a repetition of the Spanish Armada on a small scale. There were royal sloops of war and Company's cruisers to convoy the transports and—a portent which it was hoped would impress the minds of native observers with superstitious awe—a tiny steam vessel, the *Diana*, was with the flotilla.

There is a beautiful and commodious harbour called Port Cornwallis, in one of the Andaman Islands, then the abode only of savages, and here was the rendezvous of the squadrons. On May 9 the fleet reached the Rangoon river—one of the many mouths of the Irawadi. The bar was crossed, in spite of some dismal prophecies, without a serious hitch, and on the morning of the 11th the vessel cast anchor in the wide stream in front of Rangoon. A few shots were fired from the feeble defences of the town. The *Liffey* answered, dismounting the guns, and forthwith the gunners fled. An American missionary brought a message from the Governor gravely inquiring what the new comers wanted, and intimating that the European residents were all in irons and would be killed at once. But his Excellency the Governor did not wait for a reply. When the troops took possession of the town, the only persons they found there were this little band of strangers—eight traders or pilots of British origin, two missionaries, an American and a Greek. The fire from the ships had interrupted the execution. If the Burmese authorities were taken unawares, they knew at any rate what they had to do. It was the Burning of Moscow over again. The most stubborn resistance would not have been more embarrassing to the invaders. Our troops held the town, but there was little in it worth capture. The non-combatant population, through whom the English General had calculated on getting the daily necessaries of life for his force, had disappeared; never did victors feel more dejected.

CHAPTER V

The Burmese War: the Defence of Rangoon and Conquest of Arakan

Rangoon had been built by the mighty hunter Alompra, in part to commemorate his victories in Pegu, but mainly with a prescient desire to secure for Burma the advantage of foreign trade. The town lay on the left bank of the river; on the other three sides it was protected by a wet ditch. The four main streets were lined with huts of bamboo and matting, raised on piles, for the site of Rangoon was then a swamp. A few brick houses, of the poorest construction, attested the presence of the motley foreign element. Some of these strangers were in the employ of the native government. The day of the arrival of the English about 40,000 people were dwelling in the place, of whom 1,500 were priests and acolytes, attached to the neighbouring pagodas. Between it and the sea was a dead flat, of swampy jungle, varied by paddy fields. But on a low range of hills two miles to the north showed grandly the Holy Place of the Burmese—the great Pagoda of Shwe Dagon Prah. To this a road leads from the town, shaded by splendid trees—mangoes, cocoa palms, and many another of majestic form. At the end of this stately avenue rose the Pagoda, crowning an eminence. Of solid brick throughout, it was covered with gilding which glittered in the sunshine. Minor temples or monasteries flanked the sacred way, huge griffins standing guard at the entrance of each. Such was the jumble of splendour and squalor in which the army was now quartered.

The Pagoda was of the most respectable antiquity. The height ascended from the lowest level by two gigantic terraces, which formed a quadrangular base for the solid dome that occupies the centre. At the top it tapers gradually till it ends in a slender pinnacle almost as high as the body of the dome; at the end of this is the Tee, the mystic umbrella which denotes the shelter under which the true Buddhist lives and the eternal lordship of his faith. The tinkling of small bells from the lofty pinnacle alone represented for the intruding soldiery the worship of the shrine from which priests and devotees alike had fled.

The height of the pile is given as 300 feet. Scattered over the terraces, and at the base, were sacred buildings, many of which were in themselves imposing and exquisite specimens of Burmese art. Generation after generation had in this way paid their homage to the spot where under this enormous cairn rested the revered relics of the last four Buddhas. But, for the moment, the interest of the place in the eyes of the quartermaster-general's department lay in its defensible strength and its comparatively salubrious position. The view from the parapets was superb. On the north-eastern horizon were seen the hills by which the Sit-taung river flowed, and between stretched a rich plain through which the branches of the Irawadi found their way to the sea; to the south lay the Fort and Pagoda of Syriam, the old city familiar in the dingy romance of early European enterprise. Below flowed the Rangoon river, now crowded with shipping; on the other bank was the town of Dala, and almost at the foot of the Pagoda lay a beautiful lake. But the contemplation of the landscape was not an unmixed pleasure. Columns of smoke ascending from the thick woods which broke the plain indicated the spots where the Burmese soldiers were already preparing their stockades. The country round was almost impracticable for the movements of regular troops. Reconnaissances were sent out to explore and, if possible, to tempt back the fugitive inhabitants. A little expedition in boats from the ships of war gallantly stormed an unfinished stockade at Kemendin, about six miles up stream. A more serious advance into the interior by land resulted only in illustrating the marvellous alacrity with which the villagers could disappear into the jungle, and in leaving our commanders with two gilt umbrellas as the first trophies of war. A number of mutilated bodies were found in the wood, a sample of the terrors by which unswerving loyalty to the crown of Ava was maintained. In May the dreaded rains set in, and the garrison found itself beleaguered by the floods. To conduct the force up 500 miles of stream in open boats under this tropical downpour would have been madness, even if boats could have been obtained. As to the route by land, the inundations were a fatal impediment. Nor was there available carriage, nor prospect of supplies. The Burmese authorities had rendered Sir Eyre Coote's primitive system of commissariat impracticable by the simple plan of making the country a desert in the track of our troops. There was nothing for it but to wait till the rains were over, and meanwhile to draw supplies from Calcutta and Madras. There was happily no difficulty about making the necessary dispositions for the defence of Rangoon in the very improbable contingency of an attack. Nor was the hope abandoned that when the people of Pegu had realized the discomfiture of the Burmese oppressor they would declare on the side of the British. But since the days when Alompra finally asserted the supremacy of Ava over Pegu, the policy of the Burmese had been ingeniously directed to discouraging and supplanting all that was national in the old race. These people, the Talaings, were a standing exception to the doctrine that force is no remedy for disaffection. They had been thoroughly cowed into acceptance of the alien rule.

We have now to turn from the offensive operations of the war to those in Assam and Cachar, and on the Arakan frontier, which were in their primary purpose defensive. The cruelty of the Burmese conquerors in

Assam had left the population sufficient spirit to resent the wrongs they endured, and here, at any rate, our forces received a welcome, but that was really all that the people had it in their power to bestow. Our banners advanced along the Brahmaputra from Goálpárá to Gauháti, but the rains in this quarter also compelled our commanders to rest. It was the same in Cachar. There too the Burmese remained in occupation.

It would have been well if nothing worse had occurred on the Arakanese side than the maintenance of the *status quo.* Something had been done to augment the scanty force of the Company by the enrolment of a Mug levy, but Maha Bandúla had discerned with unerring eye the weakness of our position. He could afford to neglect Rangoon as long as he could deal us a blow in the point where we were vulnerable. There is no reason for describing as bombast or vainglory the repeated assurances given by this remarkable man to his royal master, that he could force his way to Calcutta without calling upon more than the local resources of the dependent provinces. A favourite of the queen, who was herself a favourite of the king, he had advantages in the councils of Amarápura such as were denied to most of the functionaries with outlandish titles among whom executive authority was frittered away. He obtained permission to lead an army of more than 10,000 men through Arakan to Chittagong. It reached the British frontier in May about the time that Sir Archibald Campbell occupied Rangoon. Crossing the Náf it advanced to within fourteen miles of Rámu, an advanced post held by a body of a few hundred of the Company's Infantry, supplemented by some of the ill-trained and unreliable Mugs. For a time the position was held courageously enough as the 8,000 Burmese combatants advanced in their traditional style, each man digging his own shelter-hole in the ground, until they reached the pickets. Then our position being plainly untenable, a retreat was ordered, but when the Sepoys reached a stream which crossed the way and the enemy pressed close upon their rear they became utterly demoralized, flinging away their arms and rushing tumultuously into the water. There were deplorable casualties amongst the British officers, and more than half of the rank and file were missing. Some of our soldiers were taken as prisoners to the Burmese capital, where their appearance was held to justify Bandúla's confidence in his star. In our own territories too the disaster caused a panic, at which we may now afford to smile, but which was then not wholly unjustified by the possibilities of the case. Fortunately the Golden Foot found itself uncomfortably pinched by the presence of our garrison at Rangoon. Bandúla with the flower of his army was recalled to expel the impudent intruders in the south, and on our side the reinforcements were tardily sent to Chittagong which should have been there at the outset.

One operation of some importance was carried out with entire success. When the fleets met at Port Cornwallis a portion of the force was sent to reduce Cheduba, one of the numerous islands which fringe the Arakanese coast. The Rájá was captured in the jungle and sent as a prisoner with his wife to Calcutta, where the Burmese princess—as has been seen from the diary—became an object of interest and kindly sympathy to the great lady, the wife of the Governor-General.

A small garrison was left in the island, which became a position of diplomatic rather than of strategic interest. We return to Rangoon, where the troops had been placed in defensive positions at the Pagoda and along the Causeway connecting it with the town. The discomfort caused by the rains was much enhanced by the failure of provisions, and by the beginning of June there was nothing but salt meat, for the most part, putrid, even for the invalids in the hospital. Vegetables there were none, and though tempting gardens of pine apples lay outside the lines, the fruit could only be gathered by armed bodies of men. The incessant attacks kept up in guerilla fashion by the Burmese bands who lurked in the country round were almost welcome as a distraction from these monotonous privations. The first experience of fire-rafts—of which much had in a vague way been heard before—was exciting. These were a series of bamboo platforms loosely hinged, so that when they struck the shipping, they easily closed round the hulls. On these floating floors were piled jars of mineral oil and every variety of combustible, from which so fierce and high was the blaze that the observers at the Pagoda trembled for the safety of the fleet. Happily the naval officers learned betimes the knack of arresting the rafts by beams across the river and converting the monsters into harmless bonfires.

Far more formidable was the land system of stockades with which in frequent sallies and expeditions the garrison soon made acquaintance. They varied in size and elaboration, but one general description may suffice for all. The unvarying element was a continuous wall, sometimes as high as twenty feet, of solid timber—the stem of bamboos or trunks of saplings from the neighbouring forests. At the top ran horizontal beams which held all firmly together. At intervals were loopholes for musketry fire. Within the enclosure, which was square or oblong, were raised platforms of earth or wood from which small guns could discharge over the paling. Inside and outside the stockade were trenches, and on the external face were often abattis formed of trunks of trees. Such was the Burmese arrangement for defence, and a modification of the system served for attack. It is hardly an exaggeration to say that the Burmese combatants operated underground. While they were still at a distance our officers saw them advancing in regular line, but presently the units that formed the rank were prostrate on the ground, and before long they were all comfortably ensconced in couples in small excavations something after the manner of the pit dwellings of prehistoric times. Even a roof was not wanting, and each couple of soldiers had with them the simple commissariat necessary for the whole period during which the siege was expected to last.

It was not long before the English leaders found a way of coping with the difficulties of this novel system of warfare. A cannonade was almost useless against the stockades: the very flimsiness of the structure was its strength. But shells had a wonderful effect in unnerving the defenders, while at least the European soldiers developed a marvellous capacity for climbing and swarming over the barrier. The courage of the natives did not long survive the consciousness that their position was no longer impregnable, and though in the very early stage of hostilities the barbarous shouts and yells and drummings of the warriors of Ava unmanned the assailants, there came a time when the mere appearance of the soldiers of John Company rushing to the attack on one side, was the signal for a wholesale flight of the Burmese on the other. The capture of a stockade was sometimes like a hurdle race, but occasionally the conflict was desperate and there were cases in which victory remained with the less civilized combatants. To the last it was considered unsafe to send Sepoys against the enclosures unless they were supported or even led by Europeans. Many contemporaneous sketches exist of these encounters, which give a vivid picture of the romantic contrasts of the war. We see the men of the king's or the Company's regiments with their tall stiff hats, their straight-cut coats, their closely-fitting breeches, and well-kept accoutrements, descending from the palisade with a haste which the artist of the time has made consistent with unruffled dignity. The bayonet is plied, the smoke of the discharges goes up to the sky in white puffs. On the other side are the unfortunate Burmese, some resisting as best they may with their broad swords, but most rushing away in confused rout. Above the parapet of the palisade appear the waving palms and the rich forest foliage—the peaceful setting of this scene of bloodshed.

But it must not be supposed that the Burmese soldiery were a barbarous rabble. As marksmen they took accurate aim, though their weapons and ammunition were of the most wretched kind. They had, however, some excellent guns, a fact for which the invaders were quite unprepared. Nor were they wanting in the proprieties of uniform. A black glazed jacket, a silk band round the waist, a silk scarf over the shoulder, a red fillet round the hair which was tied in a knot at the top of the head, a sword slung over the arm, a spear, a musket, a powder-horn and a shot-pouch completed the equipment. In justice to the enemy it should be said, that though in masses they often fled, as individuals they showed an absolute contempt of death. But the bitterest feelings of resentment were stirred among our troops by the evidence which presented itself of their cruelty to the wounded, and of the horrible indignities they offered to the dead. It may be that the man who holds his own life cheap is courageous, not from heroism but from insensibility.

We cannot attempt to chronicle in detail the events of this dreary year. Operations were necessarily confined to the country about Rangoon. Kemendin, as the starting-point of the fire-rafts, had to be taken. Very gallantly the work was done. A detachment was sent also to drive the enemy from the fort at Syriam. Later on there was another expedition to Pegu, the ancient capital of the province. Eighty years before it had been a splendid and opulent city: now it was an almost desolate ruin. Such is history in the East. These places were accessible by the network of river branches in the centre of which Rangoon lies. An attack on a stockaded post of the Burmese at Kaik-lo ended in a check for the British—the news of which was received with great delight at Amarápura. In some later marches our soldiers were sickened by the sight of the bodies of their comrades who fell, hanging mutilated and gibbeted on trees. There is too much reason to fear that a sense of jealousy or soreness led to this failure. The attack was left to the Madras Sepoys; and being unsupported they were repulsed. The hardships endured by the troops on all these occasions were extreme. The floods were out: there were no roads, hardly indeed tracks: cannon could not be moved.

When they bivouacked, mud was the soldier's bed, a log his pillow. Only a portion of the garrison was fit for service. Sickness raged in the cantonment.

No information, meanwhile, could be obtained of the movements of the enemy beyond the points of occasional contact with the scattered bands or posts. As a matter of fact, our comrades had, as yet, to deal only with raw local levies. For Bandúla's grand army had not come baçk from Arakan, and the host organized at the capital to expel the insolent strangers was still on the way. The very crudity of Burmese organization made it an easy matter to extemporize a militia. The local governor knew he would answer with his head if he failed, and the masses of the people were creatures of his will. An elaborate cordon of guard-houses prevented any approach to our lines. But by degrees about 200 were able to make their way in, chiefly to serve as menial servants.

There were a number of small excitements to prevent time from hanging heavily on the hands of Sir Archibald Campbell and his staff. The smartest captain on board the men-of-war could not help admiring the easy sweep of the war-boats which brought down messages in the king's name to the intruders, or rather inquiries as to what they wanted on the territory of the Monarch of Monarchs. Outside of Norse legends nothing could be more stately and graceful than these colossal canoes, with their trim crews of scores of oarsmen. Then there was the awful yelling from the jungles at night, and marvellous stories to tell of clever thefts and of sudden attacks upon the gunboats. In August a great body of devotees, who styled themselves Invulnerables, and had certainly gone through a course of magical preparation that ought to have insured immunity, made some daring efforts to free the Holy Pagoda from the profanation of our presence.

One visitor was a particularly interesting personage—a man named Gibson, who, born at Madras, the son of an English father and native mother, had ingratiated himself with the Court of Ava, and had, before the outbreak of war, been sent to Cochin China to arrange for a combined attack by the two States on Siam. On his return he found, much to his surprise, that his countrymen were installed at Rangoon. He is described as a man of extraordinary attainments in everything that concerns the East, in addition to which he spoke English, Portuguese, and a little French. But he was especially welcome because he had a map of Burma in his possession: and was thus able at last to furnish the Intelligence Department with the rudiments of information.

But the season was by no means wasted. The forced inactivity on the Irawadi enabled the commander to send off small expeditions by sea to capture Mergui and Tavoy, Martaban and Ye—ports of much value on the long coastline of Tenasserim. We have already described the fluctuating character of possession in these tracts. Tenasserim had for only twenty years acknowledged the supremacy of Ava, and the people had not the smallest objection to exchange of masters. Although these conquests were only subsidiary to the main object of the campaign, they remained a part of the solid fruits of our ultimate triumph.

We may perhaps add here that, partly owing to the withdrawal of the Burmese armies, and partly owing to the advantages we enjoyed by the command of local allies (whose battle we were really fighting), we had succeeded by the middle of 1825 in effacing the last traces of Burmese power in Assam, Cachar, and Manipur.

In spite of the spasmodic elation produced by the accounts of occasional British reverses and the arrival of prisoners and captured arms, the King of Ava, and what was more, the Queen, were conscious that things were not going well in the South. All hopes were now centred in Bandúla. When the Prince of Tharawadi, whom he superseded, made over the command to him at Donabyú, he gave the plebeian general some cautions, out of the fund of his own experience, as to the danger of despising the might of 'the strangers.' 'In eight days,' was the reply, 'I shall dine in the public hall'—which by the way was a sort of barn—'and afterwards return thanks'—the Burmese equivalent for a *Te Deum*—'at the Shwe Dagon Pagoda.' Inspired with this confidence, he marched down the left bank with the better part of his army of 60,000 men; a force which included a contingent of cavalry, mounted on ponies. Four days sufficed to place the host in front of the British position. The garrison numbered then 1,300 British effectives and 2,500 of the native Indian regiments. On the river was a fleet of Burmese war-ships, and the usual provision of fire-rafts. The Pagoda and the outpost at Kemendin were the principal objects menaced. But after some successful preliminary sorties, a combined attack was made by the British with the help of their gunboats on the Burmese entrenchments. The enemy's lines were carried and the soldiers of Ava fled, leaving their banners, umbrellas, and much munition of war to the victors. This was on December 6, 1824. A week later, two miles from the Pagoda, a stockade at which Bandúla had made a stand was taken, and the Burmese commander, accepting his first defeat, retired to the fortified position he had prepared at Donabyú.

In these operations the flotilla had done much service, and the little steamer *Diana* had demonstrated for the first time in eastern waters the value of steam in naval warfare. The Governor-General's bodyguard, which had under the stress of the situation been despatched from Calcutta, had, like our own guardsmen in similar circumstances, behaved with conspicuous courage. A great conflagration within the British lines at a critical moment was happily extinguished.

The retreat of the Burmese marked the close of the period of inaction in Pegu. Meanwhile energetic measures were being taken in the original seat of the troubles to restore the prestige of the Company. Few countries presented greater difficulty to a military commander. The rainfall on this coastline is far above the standard even of the humid regions of the world. The rivers perversely flow from the central mountain range almost parallel to the coast, and for great distances are rather estuaries than streams, so that a force advancing to the south would have to pass through sodden wastes either sterile or covered with dense masses of tropical vegetation, and at frequent intervals have to cross what were practically inlets of the sea. The beauty of the scenery was no adequate set-off in the eyes of the commanders for the enormous difficulties of transport. As will be seen hereafter the Government at Calcutta found the gravity of their task aggravated by the mutinous spirit of the troops who were detailed for the undertaking. At length, however, an army of 11,000 men was concentrated at Chittagong under General Morrison. Gunboats and cruisers sailed along the coast carrying the two European regiments. The passage of the Náf river was not disputed by the enemy, but a painful struggle of two months with physical obstacles lay before them. Sir Henry Lawrence, then a subaltern, was serving with General Morrison; and there is an interesting account in his *Life* of the many struggles his division encountered on its way—Sir Henry, up to his waist in water, fording rivers and transporting all the horses of a regiment and all the ammunition with infinite fatigue! But the hardships were for the moment forgotten when the army found itself before the ancient capital of Arakan in its picturesque setting of low hills. The garrison consisted of the remains of Bandúla's army, and after the second day's attack they took to flight, carrying across the mountains evil tidings to the King of Ava.

Lady Amherst writes, in April 1825, of the painful state of suspense in which they are all waiting at Calcutta. No official news arrives from the armies till the 14th. Then at last comes the most cheering account of the capture of the capital, 'after efforts which seem almost supernatural.'

On March 29 the force advanced,

'and came in sight of the very strong position taken up by the enemy for the defence of Arakan. It was a range of hills almost inaccessible, surrounded by dangerous swamps, the summits being cleared and entrenched. An attack on these heights on the evening of March 29 failed owing to the extreme difficulty of ascending the heights, which were nearly perpendicular, and the successful resistance of the enemy rolling down stones. Pointed pieces of bamboo stuck into the ground wounded the feet of the troops as they advanced.'

Thirty men were killed and 100 wounded, besides the officers who fell. On the 30th batteries were opened on the enemy's works, and on the 31st arrangements were made to attack the fortified heights, which were the key of the position.

'This service was performed entirely with the bayonet, without firing a shot. Their success was announced to the camp by striking up the British drums and fifes from the summit during the night.'

How simply and well the story is told, and what a heroic story it is! One can imagine the English hearts beating in response to that sudden midnight outburst of warlike music.

A private letter which Lord Amherst was writing at Barrackpur to Sir Edward Paget on the very day of this brilliant exploit, furnishes us with a most graceful comment.

'If ever despatches were calculated to inspire confidence, such are General Morrison's. If providing against failure is the best way to ensure success, no man ever better deserved to find his objects accomplished.

'Manipur and Arakan are pretty specimens of the extent and accuracy of our information. By the former we were to march an army without any great difficulty. At the latter we were all to perish by fog and jungle fever. I thank God that the last appears unlikely.'

The occupation of the rest of the province of Arakan was easily effected, but an attempt to advance on Amarápura by the passes of the dividing range was found to be impracticable. Pestilence was a foe more formidable than the Burmese, and so the plan of a march on the capital from the west, which had found much favour with some of the Calcutta strategists, was abandoned once for all. But Arakan, like Assam and Cachar and Tenasserim, remained ours from that time, and the troops were cantoned on the grassy expanse which is now the populous and busy town of Akyab.

The year 1824 had been one of continuous anxieties to Lord Amherst, and while he wrestled in Council with the doubts concerning policy, and the still more serious questions of executive detail, Lady Amherst watched and waited for tidings of good. From the beginning of the year 1825 there is a growing tone of cheerfulness as the diary records the progress of events of which we have already given an outline at the various seats of war. As the lady continues her record of the rumours which reach her, it is interesting to see the facts and dates of history interpreted into this daily life and talk. When one reads books of history after such a lapse of time, one looks at the maps, one follows the march of the armies, one moralizes on the results of the struggle; but how different are such calm résumés from the thrill created by the throbbing details which are part of our own actual history, by the events in which we ourselves and the people we live alongside of take a part. Reading these journals is in some measure living the moment over again with Lady Amherst in that distant place where the pages were written, covered with those close and careful lines which still seem to vibrate with the pulse of that hour.

CHAPTER VI

THE BURMESE WAR: ADVANCE ON PROME AND AVA AND CONCLUSION OF THE WAR

THE advance on Prome is the next act of the Burmese drama; we may almost trace the incidents in the notes made by the interested annalist at Government House. On March 11, 1825, 'accounts arrive of the vanguard of the army at Rangoon having marched on the 5th. On the 16th, Brigadier-General Cotton sailed with his division to meet Sir Archibald Campbell at Donabyú and to proceed to Prome, the capital of the Prince of Ava.'

The arrangement was, we may explain, that one force should go by water under General Cotton, while another advanced by land (which was now free from flood) under the Commander-in-Chief. Brigadier M'Creagh remains at Rangoon in command, waiting for the necessary transports to arrive. The town is fortifying briskly. Rockets, which never before had a fair opportunity of being tried, astonish the enemy so much that immediately on their beginning to play the Burmese fly precipitately. As the king's armies retreat, the peaceable inhabitants of the country come back to their homes.

'Great numbers of families are returning and the market is well supplied. Every member of our army in the greatest possible spirits, delighted to be on the march to Prome, and, as they hope, to Amarápura, before the rainy season sets in. This we fear, however, is unlikely. There are several thousand bullocks needed to draw the artillery tents and the baggage, also elephants; and all will have to be transported from the Upper Provinces (of India) to Calcutta, 1,200 miles, and to be again embarked for Rangoon and Chittagong.'

On March 27, many reports are afloat both of victories and defeats:

'Some Burmese prisoners sent from Rangoon say that their countrymen are now fully persuaded that we are sorcerers . . . we bewitch their men, their artillery, their stockades, and they think every white face a devil, but they still do not talk of peace.'

We must here return to the thread of our narrative. The river force had been detained at Donabyú, Bandúla's fortified position on the river about seventy miles above Rangoon, while Sir Archibald Campbell, with whom it was impossible to keep up communication, had gone in advance on his land march towards Prome.

On April 3 Lady Amherst records

'that General Cotton with a small force of 200 men had succeeded in carrying the first outwork of the great stockade at Donabyú. But in attempting the second the cannonade was kept up so heavily that in a few minutes, having had 120 men killed and wounded (out of 200), the General thought it prudent to retire, which he did successfully to his boats. General Cotton sent to acquaint Sir Archibald Campbell with what had occurred. His note was on a small bit of paper wrapped round a cheroot and put into a hole bored in a messenger's ear. The man, a Burmese, carried the message safely, and Sir Archibald, who was about forty miles higher up beyond Donabyú, immediately returned with the greatest part of his force to join in another attack. General Cotton had summoned Bandúla to surrender, who sent a very civil message in answer, saying it was his duty to defend Donabyú to the utmost, but if he took any prisoners they should be well treated. We have therefore so far civilized them by our example of humanity. The account the prisoners give is that there are 20,000 men in the stockade, and that Bandúla has been obliged to chain his men to the guns to prevent their abandoning them.'

At this point, the story of the diary reverts to Rangoon and the coast. Major Sale, who had been sent with a small force to occupy Bassein, found on his arrival that the enemy had abandoned the place; he had the satisfaction of setting prisoners free from their irons and of being welcomed by the inhabitants. So at last we come to better times, the peasants are bringing in provisions, the population is reassured. The High Priest of the Great Dagon Pagoda is also returning, oddly enough escorted by a British guard of honour.

The crowning mercy was not long delayed.

'April 29, 1825. This morning despatches arrived from Sir Archibald Campbell with the glorious and cheering news of the fall of Donabyú. It was invested on March 28 by the combined forces of General Cotton and Sir Archibald. A rocket most fortunately falling on the Maha Bandúla killed him, and on the night between the 1st and 2nd of April the garrison evacuated the fort, stores of all kinds were taken, and immense quantities of provisions. Our loss was very trifling indeed. Bandúla is the only Burmese general who has in any degree resisted our army. . . He had begun to show signs of civilization and had issued a proclamation ordering the soldiers not to maltreat or put their prisoners to death. . . . In the centre of the stockade was a very beautiful bungalow discovered, belonging to Bandúla, containing thirty spacious apartments. As soon as Bandúla was killed the soldiers immediately burnt his body. . . . Bandúla,' Lady Amherst says, 'had great influence over the king, and his soldiers were much attached to him. He used to behead them if they were frightened. On one occasion he killed seven men one after another, when the eighth at last found courage to stand by the gun.'

May 22. Despatches were received from Sir Archibald Campbell dated April 20, thirty miles from Prome. An English soldier who had been taken prisoner was sent to Sir Archibald, bringing a letter from the Burmese Government proposing peace. The letter stated that the English and Burmese Governments had from the beginning of the world been always allies and friends, and that from the folly of the Rájá of Arakan and other Rájás, war had been kindled between the two Governments. Sir Archibald replied that, foes or friends, he must continue his march to Prome, and there hear what the King's Ministers had to propose.

'We now begin to flatter ourselves that there is a prospect of an end to the war,' wrote Lady Amherst in ink which is somewhat couleur-de-rose, 'which has been a campaign of increasing triumphs to the British arms.'

It will be noticed how again the English are deluded by hopes of peace.

'We may fairly say,' the diary continues, 'that our foes have been beaten into sueing for peace, their insolent language and high pretensions have vanished.'

Another despatch from Sir Archibald of May 2 states, that

'on entering Prome, they found the town completely evacuated; a strong garrison had fled with all the inhabitants, and the peacemakers, if such they were, had also fled. Sir Archibald represents Prome as the strongest and best fortified town he has seen in Ava, and states that with 1,000 men he could have defended it against ten times that number from the excessive strength of the works and stockades. . . . The Prince Sarawaddi (Tharawadi) who commanded in Prome, and who fled so precipitately on the first advance of the army, told his followers that he was gone to tell the king the truth, and the state of the country, which the queen and her brother' (both of low birth) 'had concealed; and to implore him to make peace as the only means of saving the remains of the empire. He promised that he himself should return to Prome.'

In Prome were found above a hundred pieces of cannon besides ordnance and military stores.

'The Burmese set the town on fire before they quitted it, and our troops could only save one half of it from the flames. Captain Alexander went up in his boats for fifty miles, and captured 3,000 boats full of the population that had fled. These he persuaded to return to their homes. We are now awaiting in anxious suspense the next accounts.'

The capture of Donabyú was undoubtedly the crisis of the campaign. Yet the glory of the exploit belongs perhaps to the slender force under General Cotton, which with ineffectual gallantry attacked the formidable defences. As a piece of military engineering the stockade was the admiration of our officers. After Sir Archibald Campbell had returned and invested the place there was less occasion for a display of valour. The defenders had the imprudence to attempt a sortie, and in spite of horses and elephants, possibly by reason of the presence of these unwieldy monsters, were forced back to their lines. Lady Amherst's brief and ingenuous account of the Burmese commander's death—'a rocket most fortunately falling on the Maha Bandúla killed him'—reflects faithfully the tension of feeling at the time. But the great-grandchildren of the victors may well speak with honour and respect of the vanquished dead. Maha Bandúla had many of the qualities of true greatness; and had he survived might have proved himself as perilous an antagonist as Haidar Alí. The suit of armour which he wore may be seen in the Tower of London; and in the sketches of the period, he looks more like a Knight Templar than a Pagan. But picturesque costume was the forte of all the Burmese magnates; and some of the most consummate knaves were faultless in the matter of armour. Nor should praise be withheld from Bandúla's colleague or rival, the Prince of Tharawadi. He had statesmanlike perception, and had his pacific spirit prevailed the Court of Ava might have escaped superfluous humiliation. But the weakness of Burma has always been the ignorance, the pride, the duplicity of the Palace.

The occupation of Prome was, in every way, an advantage. The climate was excellent, supplies abundant, and after the first panic was soothed the people were friendly. Then first the British soldier had an opportunity of making the acquaintance of the merry light-hearted folk, who are now our fellow subjects, and far and away the most popular of all the races living under the shadow of the British Throne. The absence of caste restrictions, their frank and kindly nature, their love of sport and song, commend John Burman to the good graces of John Bull. After all the miseries of Rangoon it was a perfect delight to the army to be in a place where the bazaars were bright and full, where men and women, dressed in gay clothes, exchanged jokes with the strangers, and looked them straight in the face. There was plenty of amusement. The flower ornaments of the women were a sight in themselves. And the scenery was lovely. There were pagodas and huge images as in Rangoon; but all was embosomed in hills of the most romantic form and tender colour. For at Prome, as at other points of its long course, the Irawadi in its windings forms a series of beautiful lakes, girt by mountains.

To cheer further the hearts of the English leaders, there was good news from Rangoon. The Pegu people were at last beginning to think that they need no longer yield implicit obedience to the boycotting orders from Ava.

There was at one time a little fear that we might have on the Tenasserim coast the same sort of trouble that we had with the Burmese in Arakan. But it was explained that the Siamese bands which suggested trouble had appeared by mistake. A change of rule at Bangkok, however, put a stop for the time to the schemes of an alliance between the British and the Siamese. Later on, a friendly mission from Calcutta was well received on the Menam, and honoured with much largesse of 'sugar.' But only commercial relations were in question. It was a fixed point in Lord Amherst's policy to maintain a balance of power between Siam and Burma. The disintegration of the latter, he clearly foresaw, might make the neighbouring kingdom dangerously strong.

It is now the turn of the Burmese to suffer privations. Lady Amherst writes in June, 1825:—

'Reports from Amarápura speak of a great dearth of provisions there, and in all the towns in that part. True the report must be, for we are masters of the Irawadi river which conveyed all kinds of provisions from the provinces to the capital. Surely hunger must bring these barbarians to their senses; but there seems no hope of this at present, as the Burmese Ministers are fortifying their capital strongly, and erecting stockades to a considerable distance, and are determined to carry on the war at all risks. The cessation of the rains is anxiously looked for by Sir Archibald and his army, who are all in high health and spirits at the prospect of meeting the enemy again and conquering his capital.'

'June 6, 1825. Despatches arrive from Sir Archibald Campbell of May 10. Heavy rains commenced a week before, and he had been occupied in housing his troops in Prome. The natives were returning in vast numbers; 5,000 boatfulls at one time came down the river to return to their homes from whence they had been driven by Prince Tharawadi and Bandúla. The bazaars were beginning to be stocked, so much so, that Sir Archibald wishes no more provisions to be sent to his army. Many of the chiefs had arrived with offers of service and to put themselves under British protection. One chief brought nine elephants, with a promise of adding ten more. It is saïd that the king in despair has given himself up to perpetual intoxication.'

But as yet the King of Ava has not learnt the lesson of politic submission. An account, we read in the diary, has been received from Prome that a tributary province has been ordered to raise a body of troops to join the Burmese army which is now again collecting, to try its fortune against British arms. This was in fact one of the Shan states in the hilly country to the east of Amarápura.

The province—Lady Amherst explains—is governed by Shan princesses, who themselves command their troops, consisting of 1,500 men. The princesses ride on horseback at the head of their armies. They give it out that they are enchantresses, gifted with the power of converting a cannon or musket ball into a drop of water at the moment it is fired from the mouth of the gun: this is implicitly believed by the superstitious Burmese. 'These poor ignorant Ranís must however be cautious how they try their witchcraft against the British troops,' adds Lady Amherst, rather grimly.

On September 9 despatches are again received from Sir Archibald Campbell.

'It being reported to him that a large army had arrived about sixty miles from Prome commanded by the queen's brother who is first minister at Amarápura, he sent General Cotton in a steam vessel up the Irawadi, who returned with the account that not less than 50,000 Burmese, all armed with muskets, were assembled about sixty miles up the river. . . . They had fired from a battery of sixteen guns upon the steam vessel, but the width of the river and the great distance prevented any mischief being done.'

At this time the anxieties of the Vice-regal household were divided between the old trouble in Burma and the mischief that was brewing at Bhartpur.

Sir Charles Metcalfe had no sooner started on the mission, which was the final effort of pacification in the Ját State, than from the east arrive the tidings of peace so ardently desired. Overtures for an understanding had been received at Prome in answer to a letter which had been despatched by Sir Archibald Campbell to Amarápura a few weeks before. Two commissioners were sent by the British to negotiate.

'They were received,' says Lady Amherst, 'very courteously at first, and with great demonstrations of respect by some chiefs of high rank belonging to the Burmese Court; but when they came to business they reverted to their usual insolence of language, saying that if the British wished for peace they might sue for it, and that the Burmese might perhaps listen to them as tributaries to the Golden Empire. The chiefs were stopped and told that this was not the language to be used to a general at the head of a victorious army. Then in low voices the commissioners answered that this high language was meant for their own people; we must not regard it. They added that the British fought like lions, and when the battle was over showed no resentment. It was finally settled that Sir Archibald Campbell should meet the King of Ava's Prime Minister, and that an armistice should immediately be agreed upon for forty days from that time'—that is to say from Sept. 17, 1825.

The Government at Calcutta was in great hopes that all was going to be satisfactorily settled, but they had not yet sounded the depths of Burmese guile.

The truth was that the Court of Ava had prepared a force of new materials which might easily have perplexed the British generals. After the first sense of despair inspired by the downfall of Donabyú, the Shans were summoned to the standard. No sharp geographical division can be drawn between the people of the plains and the people, whether they be called Shans or Karens, who belong by origin and in large part by residence to the wild hill tracts on the east. Within the last few years we have found how much easier it is to subdue the races of the valley than to secure the good behaviour of the mountaineers, and in 1825 the strong contingents of these tributaries who flocked to Amarápura supplied the king with excellent fighting stuff. The system of bounty was substituted for conscription in the case of the Burmese proper, with results that any students of human nature can divine. The main force, to which Lady Amherst refers in the entry we have quoted, was stationed about sixty miles up stream from Prome, under the command of a half-brother of the king. The rest were distributed to guard the approach to the capital. Another large body was at Taung-ngu, a town to the east of Prome. To meet all contingencies, Sir Archibald Campbell had with him 2,300 Europeans and rather a larger number of Sepoys.

News of the result of the meeting was impatiently awaited at Government House.

On October 30, 1825, despatches arrived from Sir Archibald Campbell. The meeting took place on October 2, in a large hut which had been prepared between the lines.

'The Burmese chiefs were splendidly dressed. Sir Archibald opened the business with a brief and solemn speech, in the same style and spirit in which he had written to them. He proposed his terms of peace, which were to give them back Pegu, for which two crores of rupees would be expected, and to retain Arakan. After some consultation among themselves, they said that when they made peace with the Chinese, neither money nor territory was asked. Sir Archibald told them that it was not a case in point, they had entirely annihilated the Chinese army, not a man having escaped, whereas now we are masters of the country with a victorious and increasing army, ready to march upon the capital if they do not accede to our terms. They replied that they must send to the king to consult him before they could consent to such humiliating terms. Sir Archibald replied that everything should be done in the quietest and gentlest manner; but that the terms must be complied with, they all concurred in prolonging the armistice for thirty days, and agreed to meet again when they had consulted the Golden Monarch . . . The Burmese chiefs were invited to dinner next day, which invitation they joyously accepted. They all drank wine and cherry brandy and were joyous but not at all intoxicated, and the first Minister in taking leave laid Sir Archibald's hand on his heart and assured him of his sincerity with tears rolling from his eyes.'

Lady Amherst gives the last touch to the comic grandeur of the scene by a quotation from the letter of an officer present.

'Sir Archibald conducted the Keywonghee[1]. Their dress beggars all description: it was covered with gold embroidery, of green and purple velvet made up in fastastic shapes; on their heads they wore a gilt bason with something like a steeple on the top of it, and bells and gold chains dangling all round the face, their ears wrapped up in solid gold cases. Their dress was made of pasteboard covered with velvet. The Keywonghee asked Sir Archibald if he had ever seen two such great men as the Mayoon and himself. The General smiled, and smothering a laugh, said, Never.'

The resources of Burmese effrontery were, however, not yet exhausted.

'On the 19th of November despatches arrived in Calcutta from Prome. The day before the armistice on November 1

[1] The principal noble of the Council of State.

came a letter from the Keywonghee breaking up all the negotiations. The king's answer was, "Let the English generals empty their hands and return to their ships and trouble us no more. They are not sincere in supplicating for peace, and their petition is not heard." Sir Archibald immediately ordered his troops to prepare to march.'

On the 22nd another letter arrives from Sir Archibald.

'Accounts from the capital say that the moment terms of peace were mentioned to the king his rage was unbounded; that he ordered the wretched Minister who imparted them to him to have his mouth cut from ear to ear; that he shut himself up in his room for a week, and on coming out of it ordered the head of the Governor of Donabyú to be struck off. All the English and Americans were again put into a dungeon, from whence they had been liberated for a short time.'

For it should be explained that besides some English soldiers and a surgeon captured in fight, some missionaries who had been resident in the capital were detained as hostages. The Duchess in *Alice* was nothing to this magnificent monarch.

'Our troops,' Lady Amherst records on December 12, 1825, 'are reported to have received a check on the 16th. Four native regiments were sent to clear a jungle of a body of 2,500 men; they found at least 12,000 armed with muskets and artillery, their Colonel was killed by the first shot, several other officers wounded—a disastrous affair, but it had not damped the ardour of our troops.'

The check was soon to be atoned for.

'On the 30th of December arrived news of a decisive victory for the British close to Prome, a battle lasting three days having been fought on both sides of the river. The enemy were driven from their entrenchments, which had seemed almost impregnable. The Keywonghee commanded the centre of their army, consisting of 30,000 men, which was entrenched on the summit of a high hill. This very strong position was attacked by the flotilla under Sir James Brisbane. Our loss was comparatively small in privates, but six officers were killed. Among the slain was found one of the Shaumese [Shan] enchantresses habited as a man. She was one of the three young princesses who governed the Shaum [Shan] country. All the letters dwell much on the young enchantress. Another of these ladies was seen to fall, but she was immediately carried off the field by her own people.'

Concerning this strange and painful incident, it is well to quote from the narrative given by Major Trant in his delightful *Two Years in Ava.*

'Being habited (says another authority) in a black jacket and large straw hat, similar to the men, her sex at first was not discovered, but when the soldiers ascertained that they had unwittingly been the cause of this pretty creature's premature death, they immediately dug a grave and deposited her corpse in it, with many sincere though unpolished expressions of regret that such should have been her melancholy fate. It is customary among the Shuans that the wives of the Chobwahs [Tsabwas] should have equal authority with their husbands, when taking the field to encounter an enemy; and in this instance it would seem that the confidence reposed in the beauteous Amazon was not misplaced.'

Our victories bore good fruit, for we read on January 20, 1826—

'At 12 o'clock last night arrived the steam vessel *Enterprise* from Rangoon. Captain Johnstone came up to Lord Amherst's door, to announce that preliminaries of peace were actually signed with the Burmese. On arriving at Malown they found the place evacuated. They were met by the first Minister (the Keywonghee) from Ava, to sue for peace. The Burmese gave up all our conquests, or rather acceded to our terms. . . . The steamboat is returning to Rangoon to fetch the treaty to Calcutta. This joyful intelligence has been very overpowering, and an indescribable load of anxiety is removed from Lord Amherst's mind. If Bhartpur falls as we expect, and our dear Jeff returns unhurt, our happiness would be complete.'

But Lord Amherst had from the first instructed the commander that incredulity was the proper spirit in which all overtures from Ava should be received.

'Till the ratification of the peace from Ava arrives,' Lady Amherst observes, 'a degree of uneasiness must exist.'

On February 5 we read:

'Mr. Wilson arrived in the steam · ssel from Rangoon with the provoking and disappointing intelligence that the Burmese had again broken their faith and every pretension to honour, and that hostilities had recommenced. After fifteen days' allowance for the return of the ratification of the treaty Sir Archibald sent an officer to ask why they did not perform their promise. They could see by the help of telescopes that they were fortifying themselves by strong stockades in Malown. The Keywonghee asked for seven days more. Sir Archibald said he would give them until 12 o'clock that night to produce the ratification, if not he should attack them. The night before was spent in preparation, and by daybreak the attack was made, and Malown carried by storm with so very small a loss on our side, that it is scarcely credible, four Sepoys killed and fourteen officers and men wounded in all. The enemy suffered severely by our rockets. The king's brother was killed by a shot from a musket; his horse was taken, a fine charger covered with gold plates and jewels. The Keywonghee escaped, as did the other commissioner who asserted that the king had sent him to treat for peace. In his tent was found the treaty which had remained there ever since it was signed, and the whole has proved to be a trick, and' (as the lady exclaims) 'the grossest violation of truth, honour, faith, and everything of the kind.'

Under the circumstances this harsh judgement was only natural. Yet we know from independent sources that this unlucky envoy was sincerely anxious for a settlement; that he positively declined to attack the British during the armistice, and that it was sheer terror of the king's resentment that prevented him from making his sovereign fully acquainted with the situation of affairs.

As the result of this engagement, booty of all sorts was seized. Sir Archibald proceeded on his road to Ava, not expecting much more opposition. Burmese prisoners—Lady Amherst continues—say that no one dare speak to the king of peace, and that one of his Ministers having ventured to do so, the king threw a javelin at him and transfixed him. 'It is from the mouths of our cannons,' says Lady Amherst, 'that the Golden Monarch must hear a few truths.'

In the Keywonghee's trunk at Malown were found several of the Ráj Garoo's[1] letters, urging the Burmese

[1] The 'Ráj Garoo' was the Holy Man, half spy, half impostor, whose call at Government House is pleasantly described elsewhere in the diary (see page 64).

to prosecute the war, saying that we were exhausted in men and money. He recommended their armies never to hazard a battle, but to harass us by night in jungles, and swamps, and above all to interrupt our convoys. So the news continues changing from day to day; we hear of the steady advance of the English, the shifty subterfuges of the Burmese. Two of the English prisoners were sent back to treat with Sir Archibald, who had now nearly doubled the terms he had originally asked.

While the prospect of an honourable peace in Burma grows more and more remote, Lord Amherst is harassed by news from England of his intended recall. Happily the demonstrations of local respect were more than a solace for the passing displeasure of the home authorities.

We are now in April, 1826. On the 5th, just as Lord and Lady Amherst were starting for their early ride in the cool morning, a messenger hurried up with the news that the *Enterprise* had anchored above Kedgeree. Before seven o'clock the letter arrived bringing the joyful intelligence of peace. It had been signed at a place only four marches from the capital of Burma. The faithful missionaries who had returned to the king, as they promised to do, now brought the treaty signed by him, and twenty-five lacs of rupees besides.

The Conquering Hero was, in fact, almost the herald of his own triumph. 'Before ten o'clock,' says Lady Amherst, 'Sir Archibald, Mr. Robertson, and Mr. Mangles arrived at Barrackpur; the joy on all sides is more easily imagined than described. The troops were returning, only a certain number remained until the rest of the tribute was paid, and some regiments were left to guard the ceded provinces.' When one reflects on all the anxiety and the many difficulties through which the English had struggled for the last twenty-four months, one cannot wonder at the note of triumph which is struck in these records. It is almost a psalm. 'The Golden Monarch's insolence and pride' are now humbled.

Honour to the victors! There is a banquet at Government House. There are illuminations present and to come. Proclamations, minutes, compliments, and guns are being fired off in every direction. There is of course curiosity to hear all about the Burmese. The accounts given describe a shrewd and clever people. Even now they tried to take advantage of us; some of the bars of gold being merely gilt copper, and some of the priceless jewels proving to be coloured glass only.

Among Lady Amherst's anecdotes of the Burmese, there is one told her by Dr. Price, the American missionary, who had asked the King of Ava to grant him a great favour—permission to preach his doctrines and to convert the king's subjects to them. The king told Dr. Price he granted this request, and he might preach his religion; but whenever his subjects were converted by it, he should cut off their heads, and send them at once into the Paradise of which the Doctor had told them.

Even during the time of Lady Amherst's reat bereavement scraps of news from .the scene the long anxiety continue to be inscribed on the pages of the diary—the light epilogues of the engrossing drama.

The altar of the Great Pagoda had been returned by Lady Amherst to the Burmese chiefs at Rangoon, whose letter in recognition is as follows :—

'The great Lady of Bengal has graciously sent back the glass altar, the sacred Kyang and the image of Duty which had miraculously travelled to Bengal. They are deposited in the great Temple and are daily worshipped.'

It remains only to supplement in a few details the narrative of military and political events drawn from Lady Amherst's passing notes. A reference must suffice to the collateral operations conducted on the river Sit-taung, with a view to dislodging the Burmese force from Taung-ngu. As in other cases, an initial reverse was followed by a hardly won success.

The fortunes of the main column concern us chiefly. By the time the army had reached Pagan, one of the ancient capitals of Burma, the ruins of which still attest its former greatness and the transitory nature of Burmese magnificence, there is a most gratifying proof that the people recognized us as masters of the country. In long processions of boats on the river, and in streaming crowds on the shore, they were seen returning to the flimsy homes from which the edict of the Palace had banished them.

Yandabu remains famous in history as the village

where the treaty was at last, on February 24, 1826, concluded. Even the king, tardily converted to a sense of the realities of his position, gratefully acknowledged his friend Sir Archibald's 'magnanimity.' Assam, Arakan, and the coast of Tenasserim, were ceded in perpetuity, and he agreed to abstain from all interference in Manipur, in Cachar, and the adjacent hill-state of Jaintia. He pledged himself to receive a Resident at his capital, and to enter into negotiations for the conclusion of a commercial treaty; as an indemnity he undertook to pay a crore of rupees, about 1,000,000 sterling, in four instalments.

A portion of the British force withdrew through the mountains to Arakan. It was satisfactory of course to find that a feat which had been considered impracticable could after all be performed; but there was mortification in the thought that if only the route taken (that by the Aeng Pass) had been known before, General Morrison and his army might have wintered in Ava instead of 'perishing in the marshes of Arakan.'

Rangoon was held by a British garrison till the second instalment of the indemnity was paid. Then, at the close of 1826, they were transferred to Maulmain, at that time a mere cluster of huts; but soon to become one of the most flourishing, and, as many competent judges hold, the most beautiful ports in the East.

Although the submission of the Court of Ava was at the moment complete, there was a speedy revival of the old insolent airs. The Envoy despatched to arrange the commercial treaty was superciliously treated, and the concessions made were inadequate. But only a very grave provocation would have tempted the Government of India to incur the pains and risks of another rupture. The king on his part—though left in possession of domains as wide as those of monarchs who ruled in the palmy days of the kingdom—sulked and fretted. Four years elapsed before a British Resident was appointed to the capital.

In the light of experience the policy of the Burmese war needs no justification. Arakan and Tenasserim in due course became valuable possessions. Arakan is one of the great rice-fields of the world. The superb timber forests of Tenasserim were especially a gain. Assam, although at first we took possession only of the lower part of the valley, was destined to become more than the rival of China in the production of its tea. Development was not immediate; for the heaven-sent administrator is not always found at once. Assam and Arakan were placed under the government of Bengal; Tenasserim under that of Madras. The town of Amherst on the Tenasserim commemorates the connexion of the Governor-General with the conquest. It was intended to serve as a sanatorium, but disappointed hope in this respect.

It was as a first step which led of necessity to the complete absorption of Burma in the Empire, that Lord Amherst's policy became a landmark in history.

Yet we must not blame those who felt too acutely the distresses of their own time, to be capable of divining the future. The war was condemned at home simply because the early stages were gloomy and almost calamitous. As in the Zulu war, the occasion appeared to those at a distance to be too trivial to justify the stupendous sacrifices. Not that the Directors were moved by any spirit of humanitarianism. The treasury they considered was exhausted by the struggle within the limits of India proper, and it seemed sheer madness to court further outlay in adventures in the barbarous borderlands. Lord Amherst judged more wisely. He saw that if the aggressions of the Burmese were not sternly repressed they would be extended indefinitely; and that the good work done by Lord Hastings and Lord Wellesley for the prestige of the Company in India, would be rendered unavailing if the native princes saw that we complacently put up with insult from a barbarous neighbour on the eastern frontier. Criticism may fasten more plausibly upon the conduct of the campaign; but criticism has an advantage denied to statesmanship, that of learning wisdom after the event.

CHAPTER VII

THE CAPTURE OF BHARTPUR

WE have described in Chapter II the state of things which the conclusion of the operations against the predatory powers had left to the successor of Lord Hastings. Even had it been possible to reserve all the resources of the Government for the necessary organization of reform in police, in civil justice, in revenue settlement, for patient effort to remove by wise and kind administration in the several districts the painful impressions left by the earlier blunders, the task would have been one of extreme difficulty. One result of the effacement of the Pindárís, as a political force, was to scatter the members of these armed bands to their homes or haunts in the new provinces and even in the old. Thus the materials for mischief were diffused everywhere. The strain put upon the authorities by the Burmese War crippled them in the arrangements of internal order and content: while the first failures on the Chittagong frontier and at Rangoon, magnified as they were by bazaar rumour, gave heart to every scoundrel in the villages under our own rule and every ill wisher in the Courts of the native princes.

A fakir at Bhadaur notified that on a certain day the god Kalki would be incarnate in him as the last of the Hindu Avatárs. Among a people who are always ready for signs and wonders, and to whom such an occurrence appeared quite in accordance with the order of the universe, the announcement caused excitement rather than incredulity. It was a case, according to English notions, for police interference, and accordingly the divine mortal was arrested. But a great band of fanatics assembled to rescue him. Happily the Mahárájá of Patiála—a house distinguished by its loyalty to the British—sent a party of horse which dispersed the mob; and so there was an end of the quasi-religious trouble.

Brigandage was more serious. Close to our station at Sahéranpur a bravo chief established himself in the mud fort at Kanjawa. The local officers were men of courage and intelligence and with the aid of some Gúrkhas—a race which already was yielding us some of our best native soldiery—captured the robber stronghold, 150 of the defenders being killed.

These are illustrations of the various forms of unrest which showed themselves in the as yet imperfectly tamed borderland to the west of Delhi, the 'protected Sikh provinces,' to use the phrase of the day—in Bundelkhand, in Málwá, in the jungle territories round the famous Asírgarh, among the

Bhíls, among the Kolis—one of the wild tribes of Gujarát. The area of these disturbances—several of which necessitated a considerable military preparation on the side of the British authorities—was roughly conterminous with the old raiding grounds of the Maráthá and the Pindárí. The cold weather tourist of the present day, who wishes to have some little variation from the enlightened sentiments of the English-speaking natives whom he meets in the large towns, may be advised to visit some of these hunting-grounds of the outlaws. He will find superb scenery —if primitive jungle and rock fastnesses be to his taste—and in the stories told by the sparse jungle folk, he will discover that romance dies hard in India.

At Kittúr, in the South Maráthá country, there was, in October 1824, an episode of a serious and melancholy character. The petty chief of the place had died, leaving no son to succeed. Some of the hangers on of the little Darbár were anxious to keep the property in hands that suited their own interests. They accordingly persuaded the widow to adopt an heir, on behalf of her dead husband. The validity of the adoption was not recognized by the collector of the district. The Government of Bombay instructed him to hold an inquiry and meanwhile to assume charge of the territory and the treasure. For some time things went well; but one morning admittance to the fort was refused to the English officials. They tried to force the gate, and in the *mêlée*, Mr. Thackeray and the officers who commanded the escort were killed. Happily the contagion of resistance did not spread to neighbouring chiefs: and the speedy appearance of a strong British force before the walls secured the surrender of the ringleaders.

The following year there was another affair of much the same description in a neighbouring territory.

In another state of the Western Deccan, of which the later princes have been distinguished by enlightened loyalty to the British crown, there were for a time a series of troubles which illustrate the difficulties attendant on the first effort at authoritative pacification after the long confusion. The young Rájá of Kolhápur, proud of his descent from Sivají, refused to adapt himself to the altered order of things. His quarrel however was with Maráthá rivals, not with the paramount power. He claimed under a grant from the Peshwá a district which had been for some time in the possession of Sindhia's brother-in-law. The Government of Bombay looked quietly on whilst Sindhia protested with pardonable warmth that he was not permitted to vindicate the outraged rights of his relative by force. The Rájá of Kolhápur, however, ultimately forced the hand of the reluctant Government. Maintaining a large and well-disciplined force, he revived within his local limits the terrors of the predatory system. The doom he provoked descended in 1827. A British force occupied his forts, he was compelled to restore the lands he had plundered, to receive British garrisons, to see his powers of rule seriously restricted, and, hardest lot of all! to promise good behaviour in future. The odd thing is that on the whole he kept his word.

We pass to a region very different both ethnographically and geographically. Some chiefs who had been banished from Cutch found refuge in Sind, then, as twenty years later, ruled by the Amírs. These princes were not sorry to have an opportunity of worrying the British in their efforts to obtain order in Cutch. They gave assistance to the fugitives in raising a force of Mianis. At the head of these wild warriors of the desert the exiles marched back announcing with commendable brevity the object of their enterprise. 'We are Girasias,' ran their epistle to the Resident, 'if you agree to restore Ráo Bharmal Jí to the throne, you may command us.' The invasion at first was a complete success, but the spirit with which the British troops despatched from the Residency at Bhúj dislodged the insurgents from the stronghold they had captured was caught by the native soldiers of the regency. The invaders were finally expelled and had to make their way as best they could across the Rann to the more hospitable shores of Sind. But it was found necessary to maintain a much stronger garrison in Cutch as a precaution against the evil designs of the Amírs.

We come now to the far more formidable complications on the North-Western frontier, where the rumoured distresses of the government in Burma, and the confident anticipation of the immediate downfall of the upstart British Ráj, had led to active communication between the three disaffected States of Alwar (or Macheri, as it was the custom to call it then), Jaipur, and Bhartpur. The Játs, as a caste or rather tribe, are well known throughout many of the western districts of the present North-West Provinces as singularly industrious agriculturists, but at Bhartpur the Ját house ruled in sovereign state, and held itself no whit the inferior of the Rájput chivalry. The prince of the day had, with characteristic shrewdness, recognized the wisdom of making terms with the English after the overthrow of the Maráthás and the Pindárís. It was at the instance of Rájá Baldeo Singh that Sir David Ochterlony, as Political Agent at Delhi, had presented to his young son Balwant Singh, a Khilat, that is to say, a ceremonial dress, the presentation of which by a political superior is, by the immemorial usage of India, generally understood to be a recognition of the right to succeed. Early in 1825, a year after the investiture, Rájá Baldeo Sing died while on pilgrimage to the holy town of Gobardhán, near Muttra on the Jumna, not very far from Bhartpur. The little lad, whom the careful father was so anxious to secure against possible intrigue, was not then six years old. At first there was no sign of opposition to his succession, under the tutelage of his maternal uncle. Only a few weeks, however, had passed when Dúrjan Sál, the son of the younger brother of the late prince, gained the adhesion of the army of the State, attacked the citadel, and killed the regent. He then proclaimed himself ruler in his room.

Lady Amherst gives the Secretariat version of the affair in her diary.

'Sir David Ochterlony collected all the troops in the neighbourhood and issued a proclamation in which he sadly compromised the Government, and began putting his troops in order, to advance to the hitherto impregnable fortress of Bhartpur. These measures met with the unanimous disapprobation of the Government, who ordered him to recall his proclamation and stop the advance of troops.'

It is possible to concur in the view taken by Lord Amherst and his advisers, and yet sympathize with the spirit shown by the gallant veteran who represented the British name and British honour at Delhi. He addressed a proclamation to the people at Bhartpur, commanding them not to yield allegiance to the usurper, and he promised that a British force would forthwith secure respect for the rights of the lawful sovereign. He was as good as his word, and made immediate preparations to collect an expeditionary force at Muttra, which, it has been explained, lies on the confines of Bhartpur. It may plausibly be argued that to this prompt display of energy the comparative moderation of the usurper was due. The young Rájá was in his custody, but his life was spared, and Dúrjan Sál professed that he desired to act only as regent during his minority. To some extent the soundness of Sir David Ochterlony's policy was admitted by the subsequent issue of instructions from Calcutta, to use his discretion in keeping together a part of the force as a check upon any outrages that might be attempted on the frontier by the followers of Dúrjan Sál. The old soldier-diplomatist felt very keenly that he had pledged the Government to maintain the succession when he presented the Khilat, though no doubt the act was susceptible also of the construction put upon it by some of the Members of Council at Calcutta, namely, that it was a pure compliment and did not bind the Company to intervention.

Lord Lake, it will be remembered, had not reduced the fortress, and it was natural to infer from the failure of so great a general that the defences were all but impregnable. In addition, there were always ringing in the ears of Lord Amherst and his advisers the regrets and the rebukes of the Directors, while the condition of affairs in Burma was grave enough to curb the ardour of the most militant of statesmen.

How far chagrin and a sentiment of wounded honour may have hastened the close of Sir David Ochterlony's long and splendid service, we do not know, but at any rate death came to release him from his sorrows.

A column at Calcutta commemorates the high respect in which he was held, and even to this day the reputation he won for generosity and goodness during his fifty years of Indian work remains fresh in the minds of many as his best monument.

Sir David Ochterlony died in July, 1825, but in

the preceding April, the Government had resolved to make some arrangement 'by which he was to retire from active employment, as formerly suggested by himself. The considerations arising out of the affairs of Jaipur, Alwar and Bhartpur,' were the reasons for this step, and the choice of a successor fell on Sir Charles Metcalfe.

Sir Charles Metcalfe had had long experience of administration at Delhi; he had left that cherished scene of his labours with reluctance, and would have received the invitation to return with delight if he had not felt that his good fortune was connected with pain to his valued friend Ochterlony. The political biography of this period is full of charm to those who wish to think well of human nature. We find the great men of the day, Elphinstone, Malcolm, Munro, Metcalfe, Ochterlony, all fired with a noble ambition: by no means unconscious of their own title to distinction: coveting sometimes, each for himself, the same post, and yet, withal, exalting the services of their friendly competitors. They are, as often as not, the recipients of each other's confidences on these delicate questions. Lord Amherst thoroughly sympathized with the natures with which he had to deal, and thus we find him making Metcalfe's way easy by assuring him that the question of Ochterlony's retirement did not depend on his 'accepting or declining the proposal.' Ochterlony himself in spite of his dejection had looked forward with pleasure to the coming of the younger man by whom he was superseded. But on Metcalfe's arrival at the mouth of the Húglí on his way from Haidarábád he was saddened by the news that the 'brave and gentle' spirit of his friend had passed away. He had not even been able to answer the kindly invitation sent by the veteran to his 'dearest Charles' to share the 'old house at Shalimar.' Not till October 21 had Metcalfe reached Delhi. In November he commenced his march for Bhartpur. In a statesmanlike way he put aside all discussion as to the technical significance of the investiture. It was, he boldly affirmed, 'as supreme guardians of general tranquillity, law, and right,' that we were bound imperatively 'to maintain the legal succession of the Rájá Balwant Sing.' In 1817, he insists, it 'became an established principle of our policy to maintain tranquillity among all the States of India, and to prevent the anarchy and misrule which were likely to disturb the general peace. In the case of succession to a principality it seems clearly incumbent on us to refuse to acknowledge any but the lawful successor.' It is interesting to observe that this doctrine was made, in 1826, the occasion for special censure by the Home Government. The Secret Committee write that they cannot admit that 'the extension of our power has in any degree extended our rights of interference in the internal affairs of other states.'

The Resident succeeded at any rate in persuading the Governor-General to concur in the application of the doctrine to the special case of Bhartpur. On

September 16 a resolution was passed, that 'the existing disturbance at Bhartpur, if not speedily quieted, will produce general commotion in Upper India;' it was 'their solemn duty, no less than their right as paramount power, to interfere.' Authority was accordingly conveyed to Metcalfe to maintain the succession of the 'rightful heir by expostulation and resort to measures of force.'

In 'expostulation' with native princes, Metcalfe was an adept. His admiring friend, the Chief Secretary Swinton, writes to him from Calcutta, 'You know my sentiments as to your way of doing business with native gentlemen. Poor Dúrjan Sál has caught a tartar in you, and knows it, I daresay.'

If poor Dúrjan Sál knew it, he kept his own secret. He was a weak creature, but had enough obstinacy to serve the purpose of a strong man. It was soon plain that Lord Combermere, who had meanwhile been entrusted with the duty of military preparation, would have to solve the problem. Nor was the feeling, either in camp or in Council, altogether one of regret, that matters were to be pushed to extremes. The existence of the 'impregnable' fortress was regarded as a permanent defiance to British supremacy, and was supposed to have a disturbing effect on the native imagination. On December 6 Sir Charles Metcalfe joined the Commander-in-Chief at Muttra, where his headquarters were, and exercised the authority vested in him to set the army in motion.

We have now to return to Calcutta, where the

contemplated operations had added family solicitude to the Governor-General's cares. His son and heir Jeff had proved himself an admirable secretary, and a most popular member of the household at Government House. Concerning him we have this touching entry in Lady Amherst's diary dated September 30, 1825:—

'This day has been a gloomy and heavy one to me. My dear son Jeff announced to me his anxious wish to join his regiment, in case the siege of Bhartpur is resolved upon; and that his father had consented to his plan, though so painful to his feelings, and so inconvenient to him to lose at such a moment the services of so confidential and trustworthy a military secretary. As to myself I am torn with the anguish of two feelings of an opposite nature, my maternal feelings for my son (in me greatly too poignant for my comfort) and the conviction, on the other hand, that he is doing his duty and evincing a spirit and courage worthy of his family.'

The sense of patriotic feeling triumphed; and by December 10 Captain Amherst was with the besieging force. Lord Combermere's army had advanced in two divisions; the first from Agra on Dec. 7, the second from Muttra on the following day. They consisted altogether of about 21,000 men, chiefly Sepoys. The garrison, which was made up of Rájputs and Játs with a sprinkling of Afgháns, was somewhat inferior in numbers, but they occupied a position in which it seemed the merest handful could bid defiance to thousands. There was a grim picturesqueness about the vast mass rising from the plain, which the eyes of the young soldier surveyed with anxious interest. The high and massive mounds of clay which formed the defences had been hardened by the fierce sunshine into the firmness of brick, while the toughness of the material appeared to be unaffected by the most powerful cannonade. The strength of the position may well have inspired the defenders with confidence. 'For more than twenty years,' remarks Sir John Kaye, it 'had seemed to snort defiance at the victorious Feringhees.' If the British had not attacked it before, it was not for want of provocation. Their forbearance, which was known to be based upon reluctance to face the necessary sacrifices, had, of course, ministered to the pride of the possessors.

> 'The walls were decorated with satirical pictures of defeats, real or imaginary, of British armies. An old native, who in 1805 had looked down from the ramparts upon the Company's troops as they marched in the plain, says that they looked like two marriage processions.'

It was therefore wisely determined that since the time had come for making the supreme effort, it should not fail for want of preparation. The flower of our army was in the field, and it is no exaggeration to say that events were watched in many a native court as marking the crisis of our rule. It is just to the memory of Ochterlony to say that he based his plan for an immediate attack with a comparatively weak force upon what appeared to him to be accurate information, that important breaches in the walls had not been, and could not within the available time be, repaired. Besides Captain Jeff, there was another volunteer in camp. Sir Charles Metcalfe, with characteristic energy, threw himself into the study of military operations, and probably before the assault was delivered knew vastly more about the art of besieging fortified places than some of the accomplished soldiers on the staff. Yet even his stout spirit sank within him when he contemplated the nature of the task. Lord Combermere, however, by a happy mixture of boldness and sagacity, refuted the forebodings. A Jhil or lake, from which the water for the ditches round the fortress was to be drawn, was captured before the garrison had time to cut the sluices. The exterior of the defences was about five miles in circumference. A regular investment was therefore out of the question; but a number of important positions round the fortress were successfully occupied. To add to the difficulty of approach there was outside the walls a huge glacis, round the greater part of which again was a fringe of forest, which the Rájás of Bhartpur had retained, after the manner of native princes, as a hunting-ground. Within the walls was the town and the citadel which dominated all, and was itself defended by a separate system of works. For a little while the besiegers were sufficiently occupied in repelling sorties and preventing the entry of reinforcements. But on December 23, 1825, two definite positions were taken up for the attack. The batteries from these opened fire on the

24th, trenches were pushed forward, and further batteries constructed in advance. The rain of shot and shell was kept up on the bastions and the tower, and on the last day of the year the trenches had reached the counter-scarp, and everything was ready for undermining. Mining, in fact, was the only mode by which any practicable breach could be effected in the massive defences. The enemy tried to countermine, with results that might have been serious had the assault been delayed. A portion of the works, famous in the annals of the siege as the Long Necked Bastion, was the scene of the first greatly successful explosion. This was on January 16, 1826, and two days after the explosion of another great mine was the signal for the assault.

'Our first mines,' says Sir Charles Metcalfe, 'were bungling ones, but the latter were very grand. That to the right did a great deal of mischief to ourselves, for the people assembled in the trenches were too near, and the explosion of the mine took effect outwards. It was a grand sight, and was immediately followed by that of the advance of the storming columns up the two grand breaches; that on the left advanced first, on the signal of the explosion of the mine, and that on the right immediately afterwards. Both mounted the breaches steadily, and as quickly as the loose earth and steepness of the ascent would admit, and attained the summit without opposition. It was a most animating spectacle. I had posted myself where I saw the whole perfectly. The instant before I had separated myself from the Commander-in-Chief, because in the position which he had taken to the right of the angle of the fort one could not see the left column, and went to a battery which gave a view of both breaches, and the angle where the mine was to be sprung. I congratulate myself on having done so, for many about the Commander-in-Chief were killed or bruised by the explosion of our mine, and his own escape was surprising.'

In this passage Sir Charles Metcalfe has modestly veiled his own share in the fighting. When he joined the camp, there was the inevitable grumbling amongst the dashing sabreurs at the presence of a mere political. But after the great day the civilian was hailed as a trusty and gallant comrade in arms. The rest of the story may be briefly summarized in Sir Charles Metcalfe's words: 'The other forts of the country are falling without opposition; I trust that the effect will be good everywhere.'

We may now go back a little, and view events with Captain Amherst's eyes.

On January 7 he writes from Bhartpur to his mother that an English artilleryman, a sergeant, having been tried for misconduct, was reduced to be a corporal.

'This disgrace to the name of an Englishman deserted that night, and was seen in his regimentals upon the battlements pointing the enemy's guns. Lord Combermere was in the habit of breakfasting in the trenches; to this immediate spot did the traitor direct the gun, which wounded a Kitmagar behind Lord Combermere's chair.'

Of the final assault Captain Amherst gives a picture, vivid in its simplicity. The great mud walls were blown up, and the English entered the town by the breaches. 25,000 lbs. weight of gunpowder had been put into a large mine, forty-eight yards long, under the wall. All the population, troops, &c., who had crowded to the parapet where the great mine exploded, were thrown to a great height in the air and blown to atoms.

'No words can describe the tremendous scene of noise and confusion. The town appeared one mass of dust from the mud walls and smoke; the shouts of the besiegers in triumph and the cries of the poor sufferers were heard many miles distant. The effect of the mines was perfect.'

On the 28th further letters were received at Calcutta, describing the storming.

'Of course,' says Lady Amherst, 'Jeff was close to General Nicolls, who was foremost to mount the breach, and was for three hours in the thickest of the enemy's fire. They defended themselves obstinately and bravely; not one man of them was left alive, all refused quarter. Lord Combermere says that 5,000 dead were counted after they got possession of the town, besides those destroyed by our shells and mines. When the English advanced towards the citadel they saw no appearance of resistance. A Vakeel (native agent) came out to them to inform our commanders that not a warrior was left alive. In the citadel was found underground the young Rájá and the Rání, his mother. Dúrjan Sál and his wife and two sons were taken prisoners in the act of escaping on horseback with what money and jewels they could collect.'

We find a later entry, describing how trophies began to arrive in Calcutta—three hunting 'tygers' among them belonging to Dúrjan Sál; also letters which had been seized in Bhartpur, urging the neighbouring Rájás to revolt. 'I will shake off the little man who rides upon my neck,' says one of the letters (the little man being the Resident). The

Begam Samru witnessed the storming of the city from the top of a turret in her own garden.

'The conviction of the impregnability of Bhartpur' (we are again quoting from the diary) 'was held far and wide, and even in Calcutta was so rooted in the minds of its principal native inhabitants as to render them incredulous for a time to the account of its fall. It formed a kind of *point d'appui* for the hopes of all who were hostile to British rule.'

At a later date, February 14, comes another interesting detail.

'An officer just arrived from Bhartpur tells us that after the capture of the place a mine, quite complete and ready to spring, was discovered just under the spot where Lord Combermere and his generals had been in the habit of assembling daily. Had the siege lasted a few hours longer every preparation for firing it would have been complete.'

And so, to conclude the story of the famous siege, as told from the domestic point of view.

'February 6, 1826. In the midst of gloom and disappointment into which the above mentioned circumstances (the disappointment of the hopes of peace in Burma) had plunged Lord Amherst and us all, arrived our beloved Jeff from Bhartpur in high health and spirits, having travelled ten days and nights without stopping. The excessive joy of seeing once more this dear son, so many weeks the object of such intense anxiety, has made us forget all the disappointment from Burmese treachery.'

It remains only to chronicle the fate of Dúrjan Sál and the Bhartpur State. Dúrjan Sál was sent as a state prisoner to Allahábád, and on Jan. 20, 1826,

Lord Combermere and Sir Charles Metcalfe held a Darbár in the citadel and placed the young Rájá on the Musnad. The widow of Rájá Baldeo Singh was appointed his personal guardian; a British Resident was appointed to control the management of affairs through two noblemen who were favourites of the late Rájá. So thoroughly hated, however, were these magnates, that when they paid a ceremonial visit to the camp, they were with difficulty protected by our soldiers from the murderous violence of the mob. The fortifications which had so long been the despair of our strategists and hope of our enemies were dismantled.

The army was now set free to restore order in the State of Alwar. The story is long and hardly worth the telling. A competition for the succession between two minors had been settled some years before by an arrangement that one should be the titular Rájá, and that the administration should be exercised by the other under the guardianship of a Chief of a neighbouring principality. In 1824 the titular Rájá took possession by force of the real power, while an attempt was made to murder the said Chief. The crime was not directly traceable to the Rájá, but when he was called upon to surrender the assassin, he failed to do so, and showed him many marks of honour. This recalcitrance was due to a close understanding with the malcontents in Bhartpur, but so wholesome was the effect of the fall of that stronghold, that on the approach of the victorious army the Alwar Rájá hastened to make his submission. He was compelled to set his rival at liberty and to restore to him much land and treasure. The contrition of the Rájá, however, was short lived. It is a suggestive illustration of the prestige which now attached to the British power, that he was brought to a better frame of mind by the simple process of forbidding him to pay his respects to the Governor-General, and by the withdrawal of the privilege of corresponding directly with the Government of India.

CHAPTER VIII

The Mutiny at Barrackpur

One of the saddest episodes of Lord Amherst's administration was the Mutiny at Barrackpur. It belongs in part to the history of the Burma campaign, but as a symptom and a cause it may be more appropriately treated as an event of domestic import. We have seen what a strain had been placed upon the resources of the Government towards the end of 1824 by the necessity of assembling an adequate force for expelling the Burmese from Arakan. To meet the difficulties of transport there had been an extraordinary demand for beasts of burden in Lower Bengal. According to the ordinary terms of service the Sepoys were bound to provide carriage for their personal baggage. An indispensable part of this was the collection of cooking utensils, since the usage of caste compelled each man to take his own set. Under normal conditions it would have been a simple matter to hire cattle; but the requirements of the Government had swept the country of most of the available beasts, and for those offered for hire a payment was demanded quite beyond the means of the native soldier. So that there was absolute sincerity in the complaint of the men that they were not in a position to march. To take them by sea was, of course, impossible, since caste scruples again stood inexorably in the way. But there was reluctance to start on other grounds as well. The innate horror with which the Indian fighting man regards warfare beyond the familiar bounds of Hindustán or the Deccan was immensely increased by the stories, true and false, that were current of our mishaps. The defeat at Ramú was magnified into a disastrous portent of the collapse of our power, and there was a superstitious belief in the magical prowess and invulnerability of the enemy. Nay, the very indulgence with which the Bengal soldiers had been treated, and their pride in the successes that had been achieved in the campaigns against Pindárís and Maráthás, had bred a spirit of insubordination. To crown the danger of the situation some recent measures of reorganization had broken up the old regimental system. The battalions were placed under officers who were strangers to the men, and were cut away from the honourable traditions belonging to the old corps. Just when this rupture of old relations and ties was fresh, came the crisis which would have tried the most confirmed loyalty. The climate of Arakan is not unhealthy if there be the means of housing troops properly on well-chosen and well-prepared sites. But there had been no opportunity of learning the lessons of military sanitation, nor indeed of putting them into practice if the knowledge existed. Sickness was rife, and the Sepoys shrank from advancing into what they had reason to regard as a region of plague. Nor were minor considerations wanting to fan disaffection. High pay had to be given to carriers, drivers, and camp followers to induce them to serve, and the high caste soldiers felt aggrieved at receiving less than the common coolies. The regimental officers did their best under most trying circumstances. They helped the men out of their own pockets. But strait-laced officialdom at headquarters was inflexible. Insubordination must be put down with a high hand. The men were under engagement to provide their own carriage, and government declined to relieve them of the responsibility. Lady Amherst must relate the miserable sequel in her own words:

'November, 1824. On the evening of October 31, General Dalzell informed Lord Amherst that a mutinous spirit had manifested itself among the troops in the cantonment, that the 47th Native Infantry had refused to march, and had demanded increase of pay, and in short seemed resolved to resist their officers. Early on the morning of the 1st, General Dalzell went up to the Commander-in-Chief, and before 3 o'clock that day himself and all his staff arrived at Barrackpur. Soon after, the bodyguard, consisting of 300 men, went up in a boat to overtake General Cotton's regiment. It had proceeded thirty miles up the river, but arrived here [at Barrackpur], as did the Royals from Calcutta, by 11 at night. Some artillery also arrived from Dum-Dum; the house was therefore well guarded on all sides and all the avenues to it, and we then thought ourselves safe from the attack we fully expected from the mutineers. Their numbers had increased during the night: 200 of the 47th had declared their loyalty and determination to be staunch to their duty, but they traitorously joined their companions, as did about 200 of the 62nd Regiment Native Infantry and about thirty men of the 26th Regiment.

'All the non-commissioned as well as commissioned native officers to a man went to their Colonel and declared they would stand by him. The sequel will show their sincerity. By daybreak on November 1, Sir E. Paget, who had with his staff bivouacked in the Green House, put himself at the head of the troops. About 2,000 men proceeded to the cantonment.'

Barrackpur, it may be as well to explain, is a pleasant place on the Húglí, about sixteen miles above Calcutta. Ever since the days of Job Charnock it has been a favourite resort of Europeans. Here was a great mansion in a stately park, to which Governors-General retired from the dust or steam of the capital, and at this 'summer palace' Lord Amherst, with his family, was staying when the story begins.

'The cannon from Dum-Dum was stationed in the park to fire over the pales on the insurgents if necessary. Captain Macan and two other officers were sent to them. He addressed the mutineers in their own language in a very conciliatory manner, endeavouring to persuade them of the folly and danger of persisting in their mutiny, and refusal to deliver up their arms. No argument availed. He then told them the dire consequences that must ensue, and that at his return without their laying down their arms, the signal would be given to fire upon them. Their ringleaders laughed at him, and on his report to the Commander-in-Chief the fatal signal was given. The mutineers instantly fled. The cannon fired several volleys afterwards, as did the musketry; four or five were killed and wounded, and many hundreds were taken prisoners. They fled in all directions, and were instantaneously dispersed. Above 800 muskets and uniforms were found in the adjacent fields and roads. The Court-martial sat immediately. The ringleaders (six) were hanged the next morning. Many hundreds since have been found guilty and sentenced to death, but this was commuted to hard labour for fourteen years on the public roads. Five other ringleaders were executed afterwards, and one man whom the mutineers regarded as their Commander-in-Chief was hung in chains in front of the lines. Every one of these unfortunate deluded wretches declared that their native officers had instigated them to mutiny by all sorts of means. To the Hindus, they told them they would be compelled to eat beef (a sacred animal), and to the Musalmáns, pork. All the officers (native) were dismissed the service and their guilt proclaimed at the head of every regiment in their native language.

'Before the troops arrived on the 1st at Barrackpur we were for twenty-four hours in great danger and entirely at the mercy of the mutineers. Had they had any clever head among them, and seized the Governor-General and the Commander-in-Chief, the mutineers might probably have made their own terms. There was not a single European or person to be depended upon, and our situation was awfully alarming. Lord Amherst resolved not to leave the house, and I determined not to quit him. Sarah behaved heroically, and, though ill, declared she would remain, and kept up her spirits, as we all did as well as we could.

'The Commander-in-Chief returned his thanks to us both

for not quitting the house; but it was a frightful scene—English soldiers firing on British uniforms, pursuing them in all directions; some of our servants were wounded. We fortunately did not know at the moment that the night the mutiny broke out all the sentries in and about the house belonged to the 47th. The scene of action was not a quarter of a mile from this house. Many shots entered the cook-house and many fell into the water under our windows, and we saw great numbers trying to swim the Ganges. Few reached the opposite shore from the strength of the current. Twenty or thirty dead bodies were seen floating down of these unhappy people. The different regiments of British troops remained at Barrackpur about a week, after which the native regiments marched quietly to the eastern frontier, and the British troops returned to their destinations. The English regiments were encamped in the park, as also the artillery and the bodyguard. Had any cause brought them here but the actual one, we should have enjoyed this beautiful encampment and scenery extremely.'

Something has to be added to this narrative if justice is to be done to the wretched mutineers. Their demeanour on that last parade, as described by some who witnessed the scene, was that of men dazed by excitement, of men not so much bent on mischief as possessed by some fatal infatuation. They stood 'with ordered arms in a state of stupid desperation, resolved not to yield, but making no preparation to resist.' The punishment was just, but the fate of the regiment was unspeakably pathetic. The native officers were dismissed from the service, and the name of the regiment was effaced from the list of the army. Thirty years later a scene closely resembling this in its outward beginnings was rehearsed in the same place, but though the awful tragedy of the Great Mutiny was to follow, the immediate outbreak was suppressed without bloodshed. Those who blame the rigour shown in 1824 may, perhaps, ask themselves whether lenity might not have been misconstrued. No one felt more keenly than the Governor-General the pain of the spectacle. He cannot reasonably be held responsible for the absence of tact and conciliation in the early stage of the discontent, and nothing cheered and pleased him more than the proof he was hereafter to receive of the return of a better feeling among the soldiers. The affair left an ineffaceable impression on the sensitive spirit of Lady Amherst. We can imagine, then, her delight as she writes thus:

> 'Soon after the unfortunate mutiny here, the 39th Native Infantry and the 60th Native Infantry volunteered services to go anywhere that Government ordered them. Colonels Andrews and Innes explained minutely the sort of service they would be sent upon and the duties they would have to fulfil. . . . They were told that their colours should be planted at a distance and that those who persevered in their first intentions were to range themselves around them, but should any on reflection after hearing these further particulars alter their minds, they were at liberty to remain where they were. To the unspeakable satisfaction of their commanders every one to a man ran and ranged themselves around their colours.'

In a later entry Lady Amherst notes a minute of the Council in Calcutta especially addressed to the regiment which had been particularly infected with the spirit of insubordination.

'In consequence of the excellent conduct and bravery of the native troops it is ordered that a new colour be presented to the 26th in lieu of the sacred emblem lost in the mutiny, and that a free pardon be granted to those misguided men whose death-sentence had been commuted to hard labour on the roads. The prisoners received the news with apathy, asked for their copper pots and marched home—a most disappointing result indeed!'

Locally the trouble was at an end. But in those old days no ruler of India could breathe freely till sufficient time had elapsed to give his masters an opportunity of expressing their pleasure or displeasure concerning his acts. On the evening of March 8, 1826, returning from Barrackpur to Calcutta, Lord Amherst—we quote from his wife's diary—

'Received letters from Mr. Wynn and Sir G. Robinson, informing him he was about to be recalled from the Governorship of India, for certain specified reasons. First, for the delay in sending a report of the inquiry into the causes of the mutiny at Barrackpur; secondly, for making no comments, and giving no opinion as to its correctness; and thirdly, for not pardoning the mutineers immediately. To the first complaint Lord Amherst answered, that the report was so voluminous that it took him six days to read it over. The Court of Inquiry sat six weeks, and the whole of the proceedings were sent off less than three months afterwards. Secondly, as to making no comments, Lord Amherst felt it belonged to the Commander-in-Chief to make comments upon a question of military discipline. The third complaint was easily answered. All the mutineers taken with arms in their hands were sentenced to death; this sentence was commuted to hard labour. In about a fortnight, the native troops having behaved with great bravery in Ava, this opportunity was seized with eagerness to grant a free pardon, and they were all sent to their homes. Another reason for censure given by the Deputy-Chairman was having undertaken the Burmese war without a sufficient probability of success.

'These futile complaints have been much ridiculed in Calcutta, and we have been universally congratulated by the members of the Government and society at large upon the Directors having nothing else upon which to ground the recall. . . . The spirit of revenge has shown itself in various forms, misrepresenting the measures of Government, with a perseverance and malignity scarcely credible. This opportunity was not lost by the Grenvillites, who secretly fanned the flame in every way, endeavouring by every insidious art to get the Duke of Buckingham or Mr. Wynn appointed Governor-General.'

It would be pleasant for the biographer to pass lightly over the less gracious phase of Lord Amherst's experiences. But no account of the discharge of a high function would be adequate which affected to ignore the littlenesses which attend on greatness. Lord Amherst's period of disfavour in England was brief, and in India opinion was wholly and enthusiastically on his side. The diary proceeds:

'March 15 and 16, 1826. The town of Calcutta is in a great state of indignation at the recall. On the last day we went to the theatre. Never was public opinion so strongly marked; the plaudits were loud and reiterated and lasted so long it was quite overcoming. Old Indians who have passed their lives here tell us they never saw anything at all to compare to this in the most brilliant days of Lord Wellesley and Lord Hastings, after their triumphant successes; everyone says it is the cause of an injured man, whose character had been unjustly aspersed by anonymous letters, as well as a faction thirsting for place and power who have taken every advantage.'

At last justice is done to the Governor-General. On April 2, 1826, 'arrived a letter from Mr. Wynn stating, that on examining the result of the inquiry into the causes of the mutiny it was found that there were no grounds for a recall, and that the Cabinet had sent notice privately to the Court of Directors that they would be no party to it. The question now seems to rest with the Court of Proprietors. This turbulent and radical body very much influence the measures of the Directors; our fate therefore cannot be known till the beginning of next month.'

On April 7, 1826, the bachelors of Calcutta gave a ball and supper. The Governor-General's health was drunk; Lord Amherst returned thanks and spoke of the bravery, skill, and moderation of General Sir Archibald Campbell, and took this opportunity of adverting to the situation he himself stood in, and of the generous support he had met with at a time when he was so much in need of it. 'He was nearly overpowered by his feelings,' says his wife; 'the applause was so violent that it interrupted him every minute: this interruption enabled him to recover his breath.'

It may cheer the present generation to hear of past illuminations and rejoicings which are almost like those in a fairy tale, in which everybody is victorious and comes home unharmed. On the king's birthday, April 24, there is a grand entertainment at Government House; Combermere and Bhartpur in lamps on the right, Campbell and Ava in coloured lamps on the left, wreaths round the pillars, George IV in the centre also in lamps, with the appropriate accompaniments of star and crown. In the great ball-room were transparencies representing Lord Combermere leading the young Rájá into Bhartpur, followed by his staff, while a figure of Victory waved a laurel wreath. Also Sir Archibald Campbell on horseback with his steamer in the background, the Dagon Pagoda, and a nymph-like figure scattering olive branches,—India, Peace, Victory and other appropriate inscriptions were liberally scattered about, and the company danced till 3 o'clock in the morning.

Rejoicings, alas, do not last for ever, and troubles seem to be impending once more; the tidings of victory have been sent off to England, but it will take months before they arrive. On May 7, the usual letters are received from the Directors 'expressing alarm and general discontent; they are still meditating the recall of Lord Amherst, and we are in an unpleasant state of uncertainty.'

The King's speech arrives on May 30, 1826, in which he speaks of the prospect of peace, and in terms of commendation of the army and its commander in Ava.

Later, in August 1826, when Lord and Lady Amherst were mourning for the recent loss of their beloved son, 'arrived a letter from Mr. Wynn to Lord Amherst of very satisfactory character.'

We are able fortunately to print the (as yet unpublished) letter in which the Great Duke gives characteristically precise expression to his views:—

'London, 10 *October*, 1825.

'My dear Lord Liverpool,

'Since I wrote to you at Sudbourn, I have put together my opinions, formed after perusal of the papers on the Mutiny in India, of which papers I send you a copy.

'I don't see how it is possible to find fault with Lord Amherst upon any part of this transaction. The acts or the omissions of his Government did not occasion the mutiny; it was put down in the field by the Commander-in-Chief in person, into which field the Commander-in-Chief was forced to go by the mutineers, and the consequences which followed are those of trial, condemnation, and punishment.

'But it is pretended that Lord Amherst ought to have pardoned the criminals, and to have remitted the sentence of working upon the roads, because it is stated (but I don't know where) that the arms of the mutineers were not loaded[1].

'I would beg leave to recommend to the Government here to allow those upon the spot in India to judge of the

[1] Marginal note apparently by Lord Amherst:—'Their guns were loaded, but the mutineers fired them in the air, and then threw them away, when the Government guns opened upon them.'

expediency of punishing after fair and legal trial, or of pardoning, and most particularly in cases of mutiny. These men have had a fair trial by a Court-martial composed of *Native* Officers, and it is but [right?] to allow the Local Government to decide what shall be done with those convicted by legal sentence.

'I say then in answer to your queries Nos. 1 and 2, that not only we ought not to remove Lord Amherst on account of the Mutiny, or for any of the acts preceding that misfortune, or following it; but we ought to do everything in our power to support him in the performance of the duty. Neither is there anything in my opinion in the state of the war which ought to induce the Government to recall Lord Amherst.

'We ought not to have commenced the war without knowing a little more of the enemy he had to contend with; he ought not possibly to have sent Sir Archibald Campbell to Rangoon till he could co-operate with him from other quarters. But even this last opinion might be doubted; as it is certain there has been no alarm in Bengal, since the enemy has found himself under the necessity of detaching troops to oppose Sir A. Campbell. But whether the war was originally right or wrong, or whether the detaching Sir A. Campbell was right or wrong, it is quite clear to me that the Bengal Government are now in the right road, and that nothing but the season will prevent them from putting an end to the war in a very short time.

'It must be observed however that the rains begin in May or June, and that their effects are felt in the country till towards the end of December. I am aware of the power of the Court of Directors to remove the Governor-General. But in my opinion it would be better, both for the public interest and for the honour of individuals concerned, that they should remove him against the will of the Government than that we should be guilty of injustice, or take upon ourselves the appearance of protectors of mutiny.

'Believe me yours,

'WELLINGTON.

'STRATHFIELDSAYE, *Oct.* 11.'

Amid all these preoccupations Lady Amherst notes with much feeling the sad news of the untimely death of Reginald Heber, the Bishop of Calcutta. The whole of India was his diocese, and the end of his labours came when in his second visitation tour (to Madras) he had reached Trichinopoli.

'On April 3, 1826, he had been preaching and performing Divine Service very early in the morning: on his return home, he went into a cold and very large and deep bath at a little distance from the house, where he was found dead. He had been in the highest health and spirits previously.'

A bitter domestic sorrow was soon to divert the thoughts of Lord Amherst and his wife from the jars of State controversies. In the diary for July, 1826, we read:

'On the 25th Lord Amherst, Jeff, and Mr. Hale all ill from what is called epidemic fever, which in general only lasts three days. Jeff recovered for a day, but had a relapse; he was able to come to Barrackpur. How can I express all our bitter pangs! Another severe relapse seized our beloved boy on the evening of the 30th, although I had seen him an hour before apparently in high health and spirits. We had all gone on board his pinnace and sat an hour or two with him at Barrackpur. Not long after we landed I received two notes from him, pressing me to send him medicine as his fever was coming on again.

We got him ashore as soon as possible, violently and dangerously ill, which illness continued with little or no intermission until a quarter past nine in the morning of August the 2nd, when his pulse which had been sinking for the last twelve hours stopped, and he expired with the same placid heavenly smile on his countenance I had been used to see . . . During his illness he never once complained and his answer to inquiries was, "I am very comfortable, I am quite well." . . . His calm and sweet temper and very warm heart had endeared him to every member of society. . . . Had it pleased God to have spared his life till the 29th, he would have completed his twenty-fourth year. On August 3 at break of day our dearly beloved son was interred in the burial-ground at Barrackpur with military honours. The Commander-in-Chief attended, as did all the principal authorities in Calcutta. We had requested that the funeral might be as unostentatious as possible, but he was a general favourite, and the grief for his untimely end has been general and sincere.'

The record of the year 1826 concludes very sadly on Dec. 28. 'This year, full of momentous events, has nearly drawn to a close. Upon the whole the most miserable of my life' she writes.

And then turning from her own domestic sorrows, she reverts to public affairs again, and continues with most natural bitterness.

'While Lord Amherst was labouring day and night for his employers, in measures that have since proved to be highly advantageous to their interest, and for the prosperity of the country entrusted to his care, they were listening to the base falsehoods, and to the base intrigues to recall him . . . The Duke of Wellington evinced both magnanimity of mind and a thorough knowledge of the affairs of India. The conduct of the war being referred to him, he declared his entire approbation of the manner in which it had been conducted, especially the attack upon Rangoon, a point on which our enemies were most virulent, and which in fact drew the Burmese from the eastern frontier, which we had not then the means of defending, to Rangoon, the source of all the trade we possessed, the only seaport . . . The Cabinet then refused to be a party to Lord Amherst's recall, which was agitated by the Directors the 22nd of last December, 1825. To this day, December the 31st, 1826, Lord Amherst has not received a line from these gentlemen, notwithstanding all the great and glorious events which have occurred. . . . I used to try to console Lord Amherst by saying so long as it pleases God to grant our children and ourselves tolerable health, we must be thankful. That great luminary, truth, must in time bring all things to light; but the heavy and awful visitation of the sudden and very unexpected removal of our beloved Jeff overset us. This death was the bitterest pang I ever felt and shall continue to feel as long as I live.'

CHAPTER IX

The English in India in Lord Amherst's Governor-Generalship

This seems the place to attempt some account of the English establishments through which India was held and administered in the first years of Lord Amherst's governorship; of the communities of planters, merchants, traders, which enjoyed the protection of the Company; and of the relations of those who laboured in the East with the supreme masters of fate at home.

The Charter under which the Company governed was the Act of 1793, slightly modified by that of 1813. The Directors were masters, subject always to the power of the Crown exercised through the Board of Commissioners. So in India there were three responsible Vicegerents—one for each presidency; but the Governor-General of Bengal had the primacy in theory and in fact. Sir Thomas Munro as Governor of Madras, or Mr. Mountstuart Elphinstone as Governor of Bombay, had immediate concern for the internal affairs of those presidencies; but for the politics of India as a whole, the Governor and his Council at Fort William exercised conclusive authority. Distance and difficulty of communication is a factor in the Indian life of those days for which the modern reader sometimes fails to make due allowance.

In 1824 Mr. Charles Watkin Williams Wynn, M.P., was the President of the 'Right Honourable the Board of Commissioners for the Affairs of India.' Lord Bathurst, Mr. Canning, and Mr. Robert Peel were the Secretaries of State who had seats on it. Among the other members of the Board was Lord Teignmouth (Sir John Shore).

The Honourable the Court of Directors included many names which, borne by descendants of those great owners of patronage still—even under the system of Open Competition—abound in the Indian Service.

The Furlough Regulations throw an interesting light on the conditions of an Indian appointment. Seventy years ago no one was entitled to leave till he had served ten years in India; but to make amends there is a warning that any one who does not return within five years—five years at home!—will forfeit his post. Three years is the ordinary furlough.

There were nearly 500 retired officers on the rolls: so that we can see what abundant material there was for volunteer councils of expert critics at Bath and Cheltenham.

The East India College at Haileybury—it was called Hertford College at the time—was already a flourishing institution. All nominees for writerships had to study there for four terms, no one being eligible whose age exceeded twenty-two. In the class of 1823 we find there were twenty students, among whom were John Russell Colvin and George Mertins Bird. To any one indeed who has had the good fortune to have worked in India these old Registers read like a family chronicle. Charles Trevelyan, then a freshman, got a prize in Sanskrit and Classics. The Military Seminary was even better stocked with Cadets.

The list of East India Company's ships of the season 1824–5 suggests many a vision of marine stateliness and grace. There were twenty-five of them sailing from Gravesend for St. Helena, Bencoolen, Bengal, Madras, Bombay and China; and very strictly noted is the time when they were to sail to Gravesend and be in the Downs.

We must imagine that the voyage has been made and that some young writer—whose name will by-and-by be famous—finds himself in Chowringhee, on his way to pay his respects at Government House.

Lord Amherst, we know, is Governor-General. Sir Edward Paget is Commander-in-Chief and second in Council. John Adam, after his brief experience of the storms of supreme power, is one of the civilian members. John Fendall is another. This year, however, Adam is to sail for home, and rest. But he will never see the white cliffs of Dover again; and like many others of those who have made our Empire, the sea is to be his tomb. William Butterworth Bayley was Chief Secretary. George Swinton was secretary in the secret and political department. But we must not dwell on names. It must suffice to mention the chief departments of State. The four judges of the Sadr Diwání and Nizámat Adálat, that is to say the Judges of the Supreme Court, Civil and Criminal. The Board of Trade. The Board of Revenue in the Lower Provinces. The Board of Revenue in the Central Provinces. The Board of Revenue in the Western Provinces. The Board of Customs, Salt and Opium.

The Civil Servants are divided still into classes under the old-fashioned titles of Senior Merchants, Junior Merchants, Factors and Writers. Mr. Brooke, who was senior Judge of the Court of Appeal at Benares, had been appointed to the Service in 1768.

> 'Mr. Brooke,' writes Bishop Heber in Sept. 1824, 'has been fifty-six years in India, being the oldest of the Company's resident servants. He is a very fine healthy old man, his manners singularly courteous and benevolent, and his tone, in speaking Hindustáni and Persian, such as marks a man who has been in the habit of conversing much with natives of high rank.'

Even now in this year 1824 Commercial Residents, Superintendents of Lotteries and Export Warehouse Keepers (to say nothing of Salt agents and Opium agents which survive) alternate with Judges, Magistrates, Collectors, Superintendents of Police, Registrars of Zillah Courts, and assistants to all these. The Registrars of the Zillah Courts were really supplementary Judges and Magistrates. Since the days of Lord

Wellesley, however, the Civil Service had been steadily growing into very much its present form and bulk. The absence of the 'Uncovenanted' element will be remarked. We may take Moradábád, which was one of the districts most remote from the seat of government, as an illustration of the ordinary arrangement. The station staff consisted of a Judge, a Collector, a Registrar, a Second Registrar, and a Surgeon. It is interesting to know that the cutchery, 'a large and handsome house,' was approached through 'a very splendid gateway as lodge.' But very significant of the condition of the country is the fact that this palace of justice was surrounded by a mud rampart, with a deep moat and four small circular bastions. When the pile was built such a precaution was 'in this part of India not undesirable.' Indeed, even now the villages in this tract are more or less fortified. Altogether in Bengal, including what is now the North-Western Provinces, about 200 English officers were engaged in judicial and executive district work. Less than half that number served for Madras, while Bombay had a still smaller share.

A most important branch was, of course, the establishment of Residents or Minor Diplomatic Agents at Native Courts. Gerald Wellesley was at Indore, Sir Charles Metcalfe at Haidarábád, Mordaunt Ricketts at Lucknow, Sir D. Ochterlony had charge of Málwá and Rájputána, Richard Jenkins (one of the great men of the time) was at Nágpur, Mr. Cole in Mysore. Major Close looked after Sindhia at Gwalior. Tanjore and Travancore complete the list, with one exception. Mr. Gardner was Resident at Khátmándu, and his assistant was Mr. Brian Hodgson, who is, we are glad to say, alive to this day.

Of the ecclesiastical establishment we have to speak elsewhere. Reginald Heber had left, after much misgiving, his quiet parish of Hodnet, and was now Bishop of Calcutta. In Bengal alone there were over thirty chaplains.

Compared with the civil list, the list of military officers is of enormous length. But many of them were engaged in civil work. Indeed, in the early days of the Company, no distinction at all was drawn between liability to service in the field and at the desk; and to the end of our rule the army will no doubt furnish British India with able administrators as well as gallant defenders.

The College at Fort William was the place where the newly arrived nominees to the Civil Service got their training—where they were supposed to learn the language, and at any rate get acquainted with each other and see something of life. The Asiatic Society, with its long list of members, showed that there was scholarlike taste and archaeological ardour among those who had to face the rough and tumble of affairs.

But of special interest to us in a survey of this kind is the careful register kept of 'European inhabitants'—other than covenanted servants. Far the largest portion of these were in Bengal. Scattered throughout the Presidency or collected at Calcutta were about 2,500, who are classed as Europeans, and whose names in very few instances suggest Eurasian origin. Many of the trades which have since been learnt by natives were then probably almost confined to white men. 'Mariners,' as a matter of course, abounded at Calcutta and other ports. Indigo planters were numerous in many districts of Bengal, though none seem to have established themselves to the west of the Benares Division. Lord Amherst gives a very bad account of the men who were at the time in charge of the factories. Two members of this class, whose cruelty and oppression led to their expulsion from British jurisdiction, had the effrontery to come to England and furnish Mr. Hume with a statement of their grievances, which that humanitarian politician utilized as an item in his acrimonious indictment of the absent Governor-General. Cawnpur and Fatehgarh—the great seats of English power in the pioneer days—had large mercantile communities of Englishmen. The trader invariably follows the advance of cantonments. There were many missionaries. Jewellers were in request. We find even a European 'scavenger.' An Englishman kept an 'asylum for insanes' at Bhawáníput. At Patná resided a jockey. A miniature painter, a teacher of the piano, and a nurseryman contributed to the amenities of the capital. Meerut boasted a schoolmaster. An Inspector of Empty Houses earned an honest livelihood. So did many firms of wine merchants. French millinery was on sale by a European milliner. The *Oriental Mercury* required printers, a publisher, and even an editor. One is anxious to know how the Mr. Lumley who tried 'farming' at Meerut succeeded. Horatio Nelson —out of pure perversity—chose to be a land surveyor. But we must not linger over the dingy list of those who lived life as it was lived in India seventy years ago, whose very memories have passed away, and who lie—most of them—in some neglected graveyard under the graceless pyramidal pile of brick and stucco, which it was the fashion of the time to erect as the tomb of the European. In the month of May, 1823, there were twenty-nine deaths—mostly of women and children. There were ten weddings.

The members of the Civil Service had their wives, and sometimes their families, living with them. Bishop Heber remarks on the excellent moral tone of the stations in the Mofussil. There is much significance in the testimony which he bears to the high character and piety of the chaplains. Stories, it is clear, were afloat not wholly creditable to the earlier race of the Company's divines.

Let us add—to conclude this sketch of the social atoms—that fifteen advocates practised in the Supreme Court of Judicature at Calcutta, and that seventy-five Attorneys and Public Notaries tendered their services to litigants.

Such was the personnel of society. But the foreign element in it was not wholly English. We read of a Milanese ecclesiastic at Dinápur, who was the Roman Catholic Bishop of Thibet. He was not exempt from the strange fatality which attended the first four Anglican bishops. After a short residence he died. At Benares there was quite a cosmopolitan community, including Persians, Turks, Tartars, an accomplished and versatile Greek, and a Russian, who had the Muscovite gift of making himself mysterious. Of the social scenery, Lady Amherst's diary gives so many picturesque views that anything like a set estimate would spoil the effect. But we have to say something of the Governor-General and his family, as seen by the eyes of others; and perhaps of Calcutta, as the background of so much that was bright and sad.

An extract from a work published in 1827 (Alexander's *Travels from India to England*) will serve our purpose particularly well, since it gives the impressions of a sightseer.

'The first appearance of Calcutta, to a stranger, is very grand and imposing: the public buildings, mostly of the Grecian order, are extremely handsome: porticoes, colonnades, and piazzas abound everywhere. The river was crowded with shipping, chiefly European, with budgerows, bolios, and other Indian craft. . . .

'In the evening the course was crowded with gay equipages till sunset. The course is a broad road round a grass quadrangle adjoining the splendid palace of government, and bounded on two sides by the lofty and handsome buildings of Chowringhee. It commands a view of the river and of Fort William.

'The appearance of Lord Amherst on this scene did not exactly correspond with what might have been expected from the Governor-General of India, though it accorded with his unassuming character. He rode in plain clothes, on a white horse, not remarkable for its beauty, attended by a single aide-de-camp, and couple of troopers of the bodyguard, who were dressed in red hussar jackets, with silver lace, leather breeches, and long boots, caps and feathers. Lady Amherst appeared in a better style, accompanied by her daughter and an aide-de-camp, in a smart carriage and four. An escort of the bodyguard attended in front and rear. The vehicles on the course were of every build, from the dashing landau to the humble buggy. Some of the ladies sported bare arms, and were unbonneted: a few of the gentlemen promenaded in white jackets, without hats. Rich natives, baboos and others, were lounging in their coaches; among them were the representatives of the Pacha of Egypt, tho Imaun of Muscat, &c. The Strand is a street which leads along the river, and is resorted to by the more sober and unostentatious portion of the inhabitants. Here were several beautiful Armenian ladies with golden diadems, the lower parts of their faces muffled in white veils, who were enjoying in their carriages the cool breeze from the river. . . .

'During this month (February) plays were occasionally performed by amateurs; balls and parties were frequent among the Europeans, and nautches among the natives. One of the latter was given by Baboo Russum Doss Moolk (reported to be worth 100 lakhs) on occasion of the marriage of his son. The saloon in which we assembled was brilliantly lighted up with wax candles in expensive cut-glass chandeliers. The natives sat on chairs and couches; many of them wore English stockings, shoes, and kid gloves, which made a ridiculous addition to their Oriental costumes.'

Time, it will be seen, has dealt very gently with

the outward show of Calcutta life. Bishop Heber does more justice to Lord Amherst's state. Elephants, it appears, were not allowed in Calcutta or within five miles of it, but at Barrackpur they were in order. 'That which Lord Amherst rode,' says the bishop, 'was a very noble fellow, dressed up in splendid trappings, which were a present from the King of Oudh.'

The bishop describes an excursion which he made in November, 1823, to the botanical garden. The journey was by water in the Elephant barque, so-called because it was adorned with the head of an elephant with silver tusks. It was a large, light and beautiful canoe, paddled by twenty men, the bard standing in the centre, who sang songs of his own composition in praise of the Company and the Governor-General, and in celebration of victories gained by our troops.

CHAPTER X

Tour in the Upper Provinces

Rest for a Governor-General can only lie in change of occupation. A few days of escape may be granted in extreme cases. So, as a temporary and preliminary respite, we find Lord Amherst and his family embarking on June 10, 1826, on board the Government yacht. On the 14th, they anchor for the night at Diamond Harbour, where the other vessels salute them as they pass. On the 22nd, the whole party proceeds by land to Calcutta. But a longer and a more auspicious journey lay before them. At last the important letters arrive from England, letters written after the news of the armistice. This and the firm support of Government seem to have set the question of his recall at rest. Lady Amherst also adds, 'that the solicitations of the authorities of the Upper Provinces of India for Lord Amherst to visit them have induced him to decide upon going there.'

The reason of the 'solicitations of the authorities of Upper India' needs no elucidation. But this journey of pacification and settlement which—had the Court of Ava been more reasonable—would probably have been among the early acts of Lord Amherst's Administration, was destined to be the closing scene.

'On August 4,' Lady Amherst writes, 'our miserable family embarked on the *Mookie* at 5 o'clock in the morning. On this day Lord Amherst has resolved on resigning his situation as Governor-General, and has written to Mr. Canning to that effect. . . . The idea of rejoining my children in England is a great comfort to us all.'

The pleasure of the earlier part of the Ganges voyage was spoilt by the heat and the fevers. Lady Amherst was a victim as well as the Governor-General.

A great deal of the diary is now taken up with descriptions of scenery, jungles, rhinoceroses, alligators, beautiful mountains, islands and flocks of storks. Various accidents happen to the fleet; the dispensary boat goes over with Mr. Luke the apothecary, who is saved, but a 'year's supply of calomel and tartar emetic are unfortunately lost!' Sometimes the party goes on shore visiting native temples and tombs and ascending adjacent hills. On September 2 they arrive at Bhágalpur and are hospitably entertained at the house of Mr. Ward, the judge. There is an interesting account of his bodyguard of eighty men, still called the Hill Rangers. Only a few years ago these men, who belonged to a fierce hill-tribe, went about the country plundering and devastating. They had now become our defenders instead. 'Their strict observance of truth is quite remarkable, combined with a belief in witchcraft; their oaths are taken on the back of a cat.'

Dr. Wallich, who was accompanying Mr. Crawfurd on a mission to the Court of Ava, also sends letters on his own subjects, and describes a splendid tree, with a large rich drooping flower of a bright scarlet colour, which he has named Amherstia Nobilis after Lady Amherst.

On the 5th they arrive at the opium-inspector's house at Gházípur. 'He tells me the opium in this district alone produces a million annually; it is all sent to China.' The fields are full of white poppies from which the opium is made; attar of roses and rose-water are also prepared at Gházípur, and in February the face of the country is perfumed for miles around with the roses which are in bloom. The party visit the tomb of Lord Cornwallis who, about twenty years before, expired near this spot. There is a bust by Flaxman, and as ornamental details the favourite emblems of the period—soldiers in attitudes of grief, and various inscriptions. They presently arrive at Benares, where they are received with a good deal of state and ceremony. They are escorted by a mounted bodyguard to the Rájá's palace while salutes are fired. The whole native population is on the banks and in the illuminated streets; the bustle, noise, and brilliance are not to be surpassed. Next day they visit the city with its thousand temples, its worshipping priests. They met the inevitable sacred bull in the narrow streets. Even the Governor-General of India has to step aside to allow the sacred brute to pass. Besides the bulls there are the Fakirs, who seem even more objectionable, with their strange distorted minds and bodies. They paint themselves white (is it in suggestion of the text?): 'holy villains' Lady Amherst calls them. Lord and Lady Amherst dined with Mr. Brooke (the veteran of whom mention has been made elsewhere). Fifty people sat down to dinner, and at the Drawing Room afterwards the ladies were 'as well dressed as in Calcutta.' The Governor-General and his wife go about in *tonjons*, and visit the famous minarets of Aurangzeb, 'an effort felt for many days by Lord Amherst in the sinews of his legs.' Lady Amherst had some talk with Mr. Brooke about the Hindus. 'You may live very well with them,' he said, 'if you are always on your guard.' The old story of the unfortunate Mr. Cherry, which was told again by Mr. Brooke, confirms the impression.

On the 17th they proceed to Rámnagar (the palace of the Rájá of Benares), where the entertainments of jewels, fireworks, cloth of gold, &c., are continued to the sound of guitars and cocoa-nut instruments, with salutes from the battery, and shouts from friendly crowds who escort them to their pinnace. There is a certain monotony in these royal progresses. Lady Amherst writes, 'The Rájá is literally covered with very fine diamonds, and strings of pearls round his neck, a large diamond necklace hung down to his girdle. On his forehead hung a row of the finest emerald drops I ever saw, his turban was a blaze of diamonds.' Lady Amherst also adds, that he himself was the largest man she ever beheld, with a merry, laughing countenance. As usual he arrives in state with his processions of horses, elephants, camels, and howdahs, and native chiefs.

The progress continues by Mírzápur, and they come by difficult navigation to Allahábád, at the confluence of the Jumna and the Ganges. 'This city is esteemed by the Hindus equal to Benares in holiness. During their great native festivals many pilgrims annually sacrifice themselves to the alligators. Going in a boat to the centre of the river, they plunge in and are no more seen; from the bloody appearance of the water it is known they are dismembered by the crocodiles. The victims invite all their friends to the ceremony as they call it; I heard this account from those who had witnessed it.'

Lord and Lady Amherst landed in state on Oct. 27, 1826, and were received by General Marley, the Governor of the Fort of Allahábád, and lodged in his quarters. The great chiefs of Bundelkhand and the regions round come to welcome them. Among others the Nawáb of Bánda, with a following of 9,000 men.

The company is not let into the Fort, but received in tents outside. More and more processions arrive with hawks and greyhounds dressed in gold and silk, as well as the usual camels and elephants. So great is the influx of strangers that a famine is apprehended.

It is only averted by the zeal of the magistrate, Mr. Colvin. Dúrjan Sál, the usurper of Bhartpur, is a prisoner in the Fort, and no doubt sadly watches these festivities from his casement.

The ex-Peshwá of the Maráthás is among the chiefs who come to pay their duty. 'His dress was uncommon—a small pointed gold turban; his diamonds and pearls were few, but large and splendid; his appearance and conversation were animated and sensible.'

From Allahábád began the land progress. During the earlier stages Lady Amherst was full of wonder at the magic ease with which the tent city was wafted from one halting-place to another, at the luxuriant beauty of the cultivated country, and—dearest praise of all to the active magistrates of the respective districts!—at the excellence of the roads.

From Nov. 6 to 10, 1826, they are marching, hunting, and hawking as they go to beguile the way. They reached Fatehpur, which had only lately been made a station, and in which the bungalows had still to be built, on Nov. 11; and Cawnpur, where they had an imposing reception, on the 18th.

On Nov. 20 the King of Oudh comes in great state to visit Lord Amherst. Twenty-two of his relations, all splendidly dressed, accompany him. Next day the English return the King of Oudh's visit, crossing by a bridge of boats. All the gentlemen were in their best uniforms. The King of Oudh entertained them at a handsome breakfast cooked by a French cook from Paris. Among other subjects of conversation the native chiefs expressed their astonishment that the English, who are so far superior to them in most sciences, should be so far behind them in that of music.

Crossing the Ganges into Oudh on Nov. 27 they arrive at Fatehganj, a beautiful town two miles from Lucknow. While the Governor-General and his Court were travelling in state along the highways, Lady Amherst is horrified to hear of other travellers also advancing along the road to the Temple of Jagannáth, but in a different fashion. One man she tells us had crawled like a serpent from the other end of India, at the rate of a mile a day, and had been a year on his journey. Many of the poor pilgrims never reached their destination: a still larger number never returned, but died of fever and famine by the roadside.

The English party are at Lucknow on December 1. By the end of the year they have returned to British territory. On January 3, 1827, they are at Soron, a very ancient and holy city, and there Colonel Gardner, of whom we have heard before, gives them a review of his native troops. 'The beauty of the horsemanship was past expression, their feats of activity were astonishing.'

We may here break the thread of Lady Amherst's narrative to explain the political aspect of this visit to the capital of Oudh. Ghází-ud-dín Haidar was by no means the worst of the line of Wazírs; he had scholarlike tastes, and, though a wine-bibber and self-indulgent, had a certain amount of statesmanlike shrewdness. His kingdom, however, by no particular fault of his own, was the rallying-ground of the adventurers and bravos whom the *Pax Britannica* had thrown out of their regular employment; and the turbulence of some of the landowners, whose lands lay along the British border, had brought a bad name upon the country and subjected the ruler to the suspicion of incompetence. On the whole, however, he was able to satisfy the Governor-General that the charges were unjust. Cultivation was general, and there was no complaint of excessive severity in the assessments. The same could not perhaps be said of all the British provinces. He had, in addition, some very persuasive means of soothing the anxieties of the conscientious but impecunious John Company. In 1825 and 1826 he had advanced from the treasures in his vaults a sum of one million and a half to the Calcutta Government. His death, which occurred in the October following the Governor-General's visit, put an end to the particular cycle of complaints and intrigues that circled round him.

On Jan. 8, 1827, the party arrives at Agra. Lady Amherst describes the beautiful bridges, the ghauts, the groves of fruit trees, the Táj. As usual, Lord Amherst holds a Levee. Sindhia, whose health has been declining for some time, writes to say how anxious he is to come, but is compelled to send Hindu Ráo, his brother-in-law, in his place, and he is duly received at a Darbár. There is a reception also for the Maráthá ladies, sent by the famous Baiza Pái, Sindhia's wife, as a deputation to Lady Amherst, who describes the amusing scene as follows:—

'I had promised that no man should be present. A back entrance was the spot destined for their entrance, guarded by a kirnaut—a sort of wall of cloth, the same as round our tents, and so well managed that their palanquins came in without the possibility of their being seen. A female Darbár, never having taken place before in India, excited much curiosity. . . . I invited all the principal ladies of the station, twelve in number; they were ranged round the room on chairs. I as closely imitated Lord Amherst's Darbár Courts as I could in everything relating to their reception. Mrs. Saunders our kind hostess, Mrs. Stewart, Sarah and Miss Payne were deputed to meet them on the steps of the door and conduct them to me. The name of the first and favourite wife was Lakshmí, and the second Parbati. I sat upon the gold chair of state, and rose as they entered and met them halfway. Their principal lady who directed everything, and even answered every question for them, is a wife of a Bráhman called Almaram. After saluting on both sides of the face the two wives of Hindu Raáo, I conducted them to their seats, and through a female interpreter we had much conversation. They said they were much alarmed at the state of health Sindhia was in, and praying to God for his recovery, and making offerings in their temple. They told me that they rode on horseback daily like men astride, with Maráthá shawls, which are enormously large, wrapped round them; this and a thick veil over their faces completely conceals them. Parbati did not venture one word, did not even sit down but when ordered by her superior, Lakshmí, to do so. They remained till 12 o'clock at night, when their ladies conducted them to their palanquins. They brought a numerous train of female attendants, among them the old nurse to Lakshmí, a laughing old woman, a sort of buffoon. They also brought many splendid presents.'

Some little time later Lady Amherst received a translation of the account of this interview given in a Gwalior vernacular paper—the *Court Journal*, let us call it.

'On the evening appointed my wives proceeded to the house. Lady Amherst deputed some ladies to meet them, and conduct them into the Zenana. After taking their seats, mutual inquiries after each other's health having been made, some pleasing conversation on various topics ensued, after which the party was entertained by the singing of some English Nautch girls. The visit lasted three hours, when my wives took occasion to present to Lady Amherst the articles which they had brought with them for that purpose, viz. a female elephant, twenty-four trays of jewels, and twenty-seven trays of muslin, &c., which her ladyship did them the honour to accept. After expressing her approval of the elephant, Lady Amherst said she would eat the air upon it (take an airing upon it) the following day. Her ladyship presented them with atr and pawn, and conducted them to the lip of the carpet. The English Nautch girls,' says Lady Amherst, 'were no less than Sarah and Miss Payne, who had been presented to Lakshmí by name. I told them that in England it was the custom for young ladies of rank to occupy themselves constantly, and music was studied by them and was one of their amusements.'

A little further on we get the wives' own account of the visit, which is very characteristic. It is a translation from the Persian of a letter from Lakshmí Bái to the Baiza Bái.

'On our arrival at the house we found that a high wall of cloth had been placed round the door on every side and all necessary precautions taken, that none of us might be polluted by the fame-destroying eyes of the English Sáhibs. Two ladies were sent to conduct us to the Zenana. I was so much agitated at approaching the great lady that I could hardly breathe. For some time I was hardly able to lift my eyes to her countenance, which was dazzling as the sun at noonday. After making the usual salutations and inquiring after each other's health we sat down. The great lady was sitting on a golden Musnid of curious workmanship and resembling the mountain Kailás in splendour; she did not sit cross-legs like your Highness, but with her feet hanging down to the ground in a strange manner which I cannot describe, but which I think must be very painful. The great lady's stature is exalted as the Heavens, and her appearance surpassing that of the other ladies who were present, as the full moon does that of two days old. On the top of her turban she wore a waving plume of white feathers resembling the wing of the Scivroogh, and on the front of the turban was a Sirpesch of light-scattering diamonds which sparkled like the Pleiades. The other parts of the Sahibin's dress it is impossible to describe, being entirely different to the dress worn by the ladies of our country. She did not wear a Sary or Dossuttah or even Pyjamas: neither did she wear nose rings, which was very surprising; but what caused me most astonishment was that her throat and neck were quite uncovered. This shocked me very much. There were a great many more of the great lord's wives present; some were very handsome, but most of them so horridly white that they appeared like figures of marble. After we had all taken our seats some pleasing conversation ensued, but I was so bewildered with the novelty of the scene, that I scarcely knew what passed. The elegance of the room was beyond the powers of the picture-painting pen of description. The walls were covered with pictures of the great lord's wives and mistresses in different dresses, and at the end of the room in a sort of recess (fireplace) was a large fire which diffused a surprising deal of heat, which was very agreeable. After conversing some time two young ladies acted as Nautch girls. They sat before a kind of table on which there were a number of ivory teeth placed in a row; one of the young ladies, daughter of the great lady, struck these teeth with her fingers very quick, which produced some soul-exhilarating sounds; at the same time both young ladies began to sing together, as our Nautch girls do. It was very pleasing and soft, like the tear-beguiling song of the Bulbul. The other young lady who sang was called Miss Pin. She was very beautiful. Her face was like the full moon, her cheeks resembling the blooming pomegranate, her eyes like violets on the snowy Himálaya, her stature tall and graceful as the cypress, and she walked like a mountain partridge. She showed us her picture which was hung over the fireplace. It resembled her very much, but in the picture her hair was hanging gracefully over her shoulders like the curling hyacinths (this picture, says Lady Amherst, was that of Sir Henry Russell, once Chief Justice of Calcutta, in his full bottomed wig curling down to his waist). We wished very much to bring her away with us, that the sight of your Highness's eyes might be gratified by this tulip cheek. The great Miss was also very charming, but shockingly fair.

'During the time we were there we heard some English tomtoms playing in the gateway, in short everything was done that could afford us pleasure and delight. . . . We were all so much pleased that it was difficult to tear ourselves away till we heard the earth-shaking steps of the great lord, when we were obliged to depart.'

On the 19th the party visit Fatehpur Síkri, the deserted fortress-palace of the great Akbar, where can still be seen in all their fairy-like beauty of carved sandstone and marble his Zenana, his mosque, 'supported by innumerable pillars, his Halls of Audience, and all the edifices of Mughal state.' An old Pindárí chief visits them—'a strange wild-looking old man.' Finally, on January 24, they reach Bhartpur, where the young Rájá comes out to meet them with all his troops, all his ministers, and all his relations. Lord Amherst received him into his howdah, and the two dignitaries entered the town together.

'On the 25th,' Lady Amherst says, 'we all rose early to view the famous walls of Bhartpur, the ditch and breaches made by our mines, also the site of Lord Combermere's camp, and the trenches.' But the spirit of the scene has been transformed. In the evening they all dined with the Rájá: the town was most beautifully illuminated. There were triumphal arches, coloured lamps, and all else that suited rejoicing. They were met at dusk by numbers of men carrying lighted torches. The dinner was very handsome, and in English style; nautching went on all the time; they left amid renewed cheers and benedictions (into the sincerity of which Lady Amherst did not make too curious inquiry), because the British Government had put the rightful heir on the throne.

'On the 28th,' says Lady Amherst, 'we encamped under the walls of Díg, where a battle took place between Lord Lake's army and Holkar's in 1803. The former took it by storm. The palace is the finest we have met with in India: it stands in the midst of a large and very beautiful garden, with fountains and orange groves—it is to be regretted that it is not inhabited. The town is crowded with monkeys, which are looked on as sacred, and worshipped by the natives.' Although the monkeys are sacred at Bhartpur, we read that at Díg and in all this part of the country, female infants are put to death as soon as they are born.

Muttra and Brindában are visited in due course. On Feb. 3, 1827, they encamp at Koosi, where Major Fielding (assistant to the Resident at Gwalior) tells Lady Amherst an anecdote of Hindu Ráo, brother of Baiza Bái, Sindhia's favourite wife. 'His servants had not received their pay for many months; their distress at last was so great, that they deputed twelve men to represent their piteous case. Hindu Ráo heard what they had to say, and then calling aloud to his Mewátís, a body of armed men rushed into the room and the twelve wretched servants were cut into pieces in a moment. I asked whether Sindhia, who was reported a mild man, had taken any notice of Hindu Ráo's ferocity. He replied no, it is the custom of the country.'

'Accounts arrived to-day,' Lady Amherst continues, 'that Sindhia is sinking, and Baiza Bái and his other wives have declared their intention of burning themselves with him on his funeral pile. Nobody believes this as regards Baiza Bái.'

On February 6, 1827, they encamp near Firozpur. 'The Nawáb and his four sons came out to meet us with a troop of irregular horse, and a few native infantry, a venerable fine-looking old man. In the evening Lord Amherst held a Darbár.' On the next evening they dined with the Nawáb, and were much pleased with his manners and extreme civility.

This is the nobleman who, about two years before, was nearly murdered in his house at Delhi by men suborned by the Rájá of Alwar. We have told the whole story elsewhere.

Lady Amherst gives a striking account of the death of Sindhia which Major Stewart, the Resident at his Court, had sent to Lord Amherst. Major Stewart, answering a summons to the palace, found it surrounded by a great crowd of the townspeople. Inside, the apartments were filled by all the principal persons about the Court:—

'Sindhia was terribly changed; he held out his hand and whispered, for his voice was almost gone. He had not named a successor, but said there were two or three boys he would like to adopt that one might set fire to the funeral pile. Major Stewart, seeing him faint, asked if he had anything else to say: he answered, "A great deal," but had not strength to speak. Then Major Stewart retired for a little. Suddenly he heard screams, the lamentations of women, and cries without, indicating that Sindhia had breathed his last. When Major Stewart returned he found the principal wife beside the sofa on which Sindhia was lying, two women were holding a screen before her face. Soon after Sindhia was carried in his state palanquin dressed in his most splendid dress with all the emblems of state to the funeral pile, but nothing was said of the Baiza Bái, his widow, burning herself, which was a great relief to Lord Amherst.'

So passed away from the stage of native history one who had played for thirty-three years at first a leading and always an interesting part in events. During the first decade of his reign Daulat Ráo Sindhia was master of Hindustán. The Emperor of Delhi was in everything but form his vassal and his prisoner. The Rájput princes paid him tribute, and the Peshwá was in effect his subordinate. The Upper Doáb and nearly the whole of Bundelkhand and Málwá were his. The army by which he maintained his supremacy was of great strength, admirably drilled and well equipped. He had the good sense to avail himself of the services of European captains, whose careers furnished some of the more romantic chapters in Indian history. But his strength was his betrayal. Twice he challenged an encounter with the British arms, and as the result he was left not powerless indeed, but shorn of much of his early might and dignity. He accepted his reverses discreetly, and died with no greater anxieties on his mind than that of leaving his power to his wife Baiza Bái, of whom Lady Amherst has had so much to say. Fearing to prejudice her position, he had refrained during his lifetime from adopting a son as his successor, but after his death Baiza Bái was permitted to choose one from among the far-away kinsmen of the royal house, and in June 1827, Mukt Ráo, a boy of eleven, was installed as chief, the power of the queen dowager being assured by his betrothal to her granddaughter.

The Mahárájá, says Major Stewart, 'was by no means deficient in understanding, his temper was mild and gentle, though his courage was never doubted. Apathy and indolence were his besetting faults. He was raised to sovereignty at the age of fourteen, and was brought up from childhood among the scenes of rapacity and treachery that characterized the Maráthá camp. The last act of his life showed his unbounded confidence in the justice and generosity of the British Government.'

It is only fair to Baiza Bái to say that she probably would have gone to the funeral pile with her husband if Major Stewart had not peremptorily sent her to her apartments.

CHAPTER XI

VISITS TO DELHI AND SIMLA, AND RETURN TO ENGLAND

IT would be tedious to relate at length the details of each successive halt on the road to Delhi, where the 'phantom court,' as Sir Alfred Lyall calls it, was still ruling, in shadowy state. On arrival at the Mughal capital, the too familiar ceremonial begins over and over again, the unending *circus* is certainly beginning to pall upon one. Lord Amherst embraced the heir-apparent and his brother who came on their elephants to meet him. The long procession with deliberate solemnity proceeds up streets 'wider than any in London, not excepting Portland Place,' and so they advanced amid deafening noise, loud native music, and the bellowing of elephants, to the house of Sir Charles Metcalfe. 'The vast concourse of elephants heightened the grandeur of the scene.' The heir-apparent, 'a melancholy looking man,' says Lady Amherst, hunts, wears boots and leather breeches. How well one knows that younger brother who imitates the English! The usual receptions follow and the Begam Samru now again appears upon the scene and is asked to dinner, 'a short old woman, with a keen eye, white muslin dress and crimson satin pyjamas.' Her manner is described by Lady Amherst as pleasing and courteous, and she is building a cathedral.

Lady Amherst hears and duly sets down many a story of this famous lady. Most of them had been told to Bishop Heber, and to the blameless pages of his journal the reader must be referred. She was one of the most remarkable personages of the time. Her husband, Walter Reinhardt, a native of Strasburg or of Trèves, had taken service as a sailor with the French, and as a soldier with the British. Finally he drifted to India, where he attached himself to the Nawáb of Bengal, and was responsible for the murder of the British residents at Patná in the year 1763. He obtained large grants of land, and married. He was nicknamed Sombre, which the natives corrupted into Samru, and when he died in 1778, his widow became famous as the Begam Samru. Originally a Musalmán she embraced what may by courtesy be called her husband's faith. After his death she became a Roman Catholic, and ruled in great state at Sardhána—a place in the Meerut District, where many a visible token of her glory still remains. She maintained an army and commanded it in the field. An old woman at the time of Lord Amherst's visit, she lived on till 1836.

Sir Charles Metcalfe's diplomatic skill had been sorely taxed to arrange the ceremonial for the interview between the pageant emperor and the representative of the paramount power. Like other fallen potentates, the Mughal stood upon his dignity; and twelve years before, when Lord Hastings passed his way, there was much bootless effort to consult his susceptibilities without compromising the Governor-General. Either his Majesty had learned wisdom in the interval, or Sir Charles Metcalfe was singularly adroit. The meeting with Lord Amherst passed off most pleasantly. The king, whom Lord Amherst describes as 'a venerable man leaning on a stick,' said to Lord Amherst: 'As you are my friend, as you are my protector, as you are my master, I ask you to sit down.' And so Lord Amherst sat down, being (his wife proudly records) 'the only person except the heir-apparent who has ever sat in the king's presence.' Many more princes came to the Darbár, and on March 23, we read:

> 'All our gentlemen went to the Palace to present their Nuzzas (tribute). Edward presented fourteen gold pieces, the rest £5 each, which the king took himself. They received some trumpery dresses in return, only fit for chimney sweeps; so much pride and ostentation combined with so much meanness, dirt, and poverty is incredible. How is the race of Timúr sunk!'

It is indeed a striking description of the fallen monarchs still inhabiting their decaying palaces. The gardens are neglected, groves of orange trees are in full bloom, the air strongly scented with perfume, but everything untidy and forlorn. There is still the inscription over the Hall of Audience, 'If there is a Paradise on earth it is this, it is this, it is this.'

On the 24th, the Mughal returned the Governor-General's visit at the Presidency. At 7 o'clock a.m. Sir Charles Metcalfe and his staff and suite went in state to the Palace to announce Lord Amherst's intention of coming out to meet his Majesty; and at 8 o'clock, Lord Amherst started forth with the whole of the bodyguard, his own staff, and all the military and civil gentlemen at Delhi, and many who had arrived at Meerut and other stations; Colonel Skinner at the head of his regiment of irregular native horse, and a dense population. The Begam Samru seems very prominent in all these receptions. She is always ready to receive visitors; she says she smokes all day, and when tired of smoking, she assembles the women who amuse her by telling stories. She also had three sets of Nautch girls singing different tunes at the pitch of thoir voices, to the accompaniment of drums and tomtoms.

More visits to the ghostly court follow. Lady Amherst calls upon the queen, who embraces her and leads her to a seat. The queen complains of her poverty, begs the Governor-General to give her a pension, asks for a general order that every one who comes through Delhi should be obliged to pay tribute to her. Lady Amherst replied that all Lord Amherst's gentlemen had presented tribute to the king. The queen said that was true, but she had none of it. She made Lady Amherst promise to repeat what she had said, and added that the secretary (an old woman) should write to remind her. 'The queen is a rapacious old woman, intriguing for her own son,' says Lady Amherst. On March 27, a farewell Darbár is held for the king's sons, the heir-apparent and nine others.

'It appears that the royal family has been so much delighted with its receptions and presents, that among other marks of approbation the heir-apparent proposed to change clothes with Lord Amherst, an honour which it required some ingenuity to escape. Also sixteen more of the king's sons and nine other of his relations wished for a Darbár all to themselves.'

Lord Amherst respectfully pleaded want of time; for the drum of departure was beating at the door of the Governor-General's tent. Towards the end of March, the heat in the dry plains of Northern India already becomes trying, and all through the brilliant progress, the cool heights of the Himálayas formed the goal to which the thoughts of the sad travellers were tending. The way now led through the less settled tracts on the borders of Ranjít Singh's realm.

One is more and more impressed, as one reads the diary, with the vastness of the tract which has to be traversed, its heat, its sameness. The dust is nearly intolerable, nor do the trays of jewels, the ceremonies and repetitions of ceremonies make it less trying. We read:

'Near a village in the neighbourhood of Rámgarh, we

were met by a number of men, some respectably dressed, As they approached us they set up a loud shout with the most discordant vociferations, so that the frightened elephants turned round. Upon inquiry we learnt that these people were complaining of their Rájá, and imploring the Governor-General to interfere betwixt them. He was a cruel despot, he massacred any persons who had property to seize. Captain Murray spoke to these unhappy people, to inform them that their Rájá was an independent chief, and that nobody could interfere. The Sikhs are, generally speaking, at war one with another. Those who are under British protection express their gratitude in the most enthusiastic terms, certain that their property and their lives are safe.'

At last our travellers are in the Hills. On April 1 they reach Subáthu, where they remain to give time for the rest of the party to come up. Seventeen hundred coolies were not enough to bring the baggage and the company! Lord Amherst reviews the Gúrkhas who had distinguished themselves at the siege of Bhartpur, 'small men but active and intelligent, performing nineteen evolutions in the space of one hour, with great rapidity and exactness.' The diary still registers strange odds and ends of information about the ways of India. When the late Rájá of Jaipur died, we are told, eighteen men and eighteen women of his household were forced to burn with his body. Many were dragged from their families, bound hand and foot, and thrown into the flames, among them his barber, as they said he would not go into Paradise unless the barber was there to shave him. '*Satí*,' the great English lady adds, 'is being gradually suppressed in our dominions, for the magistrates refuse to grant licences .... Sindhia did not expect either of his wives should sacrifice themselves, and it is hoped this will have put the savage custom out of fashion.' Ranjít Singh, Lady Amherst also tells us, is ill, and has sent for an English doctor, but fearing poison he tries all his medicine first on his own retainers. Lady Amherst adds that Lord Amherst, 'who looked like a skeleton when he started, is now in good health.'

There is the account of a curious custom of the Hill folk, that of putting infants as soon as they are born under a cascade, for the water to drop upon their heads, while their bodies are wrapped in flannel. This is thought to be a specific against fevers. 'As soon as the infant is put under a rill of water it falls into a profound sleep. I mean to witness this curious operation at the first opportunity.' At Subáthu Lord Amherst received some Hill chiefs: eighteen came, all very poor, and proud as poor.

'One Rájá, more powerful than the others and more wealthy, resolved to go down to Calcutta to learn English habits, customs, and language. He acquired a little smattering of English and adopted among other manners that of walking out with his wife leaning upon his arm. This made such a sensation in his own State that his subjects all rose up in open rebellion against him. To restore tranquillity he was obliged to renounce his English manners.

'Captain Newton, who accompanied us, told us various stories of the extraordinary bravery of the Gúrkhas, who defeated the English repeatedly before we succeeded in conquering their country. The children are without covering of any kind; fighting is almost their only recreation. When the Gúrkha regiment now here marched to the siege of Bhartpur, the boys begged and cried so bitterly to be allowed to accompany their parents that a great number went, and their wives with one accord told the soldiers not to return to them unless victorious.'

No wonder the camp is in some difficulty for provisions. Besides their own innumerable followers, deputations arrive from Ranjít Singh and from the ex-king of Kábul. Their followers now amount to 2,500 men. On the 5th they arrive at Simla. Lady Amherst, who is of the stuff of which good travellers are made, is full of enthusiasm for the country. Although they all arrive wet to the skin, in hail and in snow, their uncomfortable state does not prevent their 'extreme admiration' of the mountain scenery; the magnificent snowy range, groves of cedar, the ilex, the chestnut, and apricot trees.

'April 10. Large flocks of sheep laden with merchandise come over these nearly inaccessible mountains; each sheep has a small bag on either side proportionable to its size and strength . . . We spend our time most monotonously,' she says, 'rising early and walking, or rather scrambling up the mountains. After breakfast, go out with the native botanist in search of new plants. Our morning home occupations ensue till 5 in the evening, when we sally forth again among the mountains; dine at 7, and retire to rest at 9 o'clock. This is our present life, very quiet and pleasant, but it does not furnish matter for a journal.'

We have seen that on his journey Lord Amherst had received the homage—rendered either in person or by deputation—of the various chiefs of Bundelkhand at Allahábád, of Málwá at Cawnpur, and of Rájputána at Delhi. While he was at Simla he exchanged courtesies, by way of reciprocal missions, with the 'Lion of the Punjab,' the veteran Ranjít Singh. The Musalmán movement which had been organized by the fanatic Syed Ahmad in the Afghán District, west of the Indus, had for some time given much occupation to the Sikh government; and the systematic aid which the malcontents received from their co-religionists in British India rendered it desirable that the friendly disposition of the Calcutta Government should be placed beyond the reach of doubt.

Lady Amherst quotes from a letter sent by a member of the British deputation a graphic account of the court of Ranjít Singh:—

'The Darbár was held in the western verandah of the palace. It was Sunday. Ranjít Singh himself looked graver than is customary with him. The air was sultry, the fountains had half lost their force and the people half their vivacity, and though only 8 o'clock in the morning the day seemed already closing—the whole scene going to sleep. We sat for some time like statues, except a couple of dogs fighting. Ranjít wore a very plain vest sprinkled with diamonds; he sat upon his golden chair with his legs folded up. His long grisly beard seemed to have grown since his last appearance, and his decrepitude seemed more closely marked. Ranjít frequently gave a twist to his moustache, looked around him, and fixed his eyes on the ground. At length he made a signal which was answered by the approach of his regiment of heroines in full dress. About three full companies entered the court armed with bows and arrows . . . Ranjít welcomed them and nodded to his favourites to approach. They seemed in no wise abashed at his presence, for their honours were well due. But he is a ghastly figure, and when mounted upon his high-bred steed his phantom face and bird-like limbs, his long hoary beard and withered form, pictured death on a pale horse.'

Here is the account of one of their visitors, the Ráni of Saice:—

'She is considered a very clever woman, and has that appearance. She was dressed quite plainly in a white garment, and her hair, parted in front and tight to the forehead, was fastened in front—the dress of a widow.' [A lifelike portrait in water colours is inserted between the pages of the diary.] 'She thought herself aggrieved by Colonel Ross, Superintendent of the Sikhs, and went down to Calcutta and represented her case to the Supreme Government. The grievance having occurred sixty years ago, when her country was conquered by the Gúrkhas, the Governor-General could do no more than allow her a small pension on which she lives very comfortably, but is not satisfied that the country is not restored to her. She is a handsome, oldish woman of about forty years. She told me I must be her mother, father, and everything to her, to which I assented. She then said she wished to marry Captain Kennedy, the Assistant Superintendent here: it made us all smile except herself; she said it was for protection.'

It was not only the glorious scenery and the cool air of Simla that refreshed the spirits of the party. In the last days of May Lord Amherst received an intimation that the king had been pleased to create him an earl by the title of 'Earl Amherst of Arakan in the East Indies and Viscount Holmesdale in Kent.' All things went well with the man whom the king delighted to honour.

'May 30. Arrived this morning from Calcutta an extract of a letter from the High Court of Directors dated January 17, transmitting the following resolutions:—"Resolved, That the thanks of this Court be given to Lord Amherst, Governor-General, for his active, strenuous, and persevering exertions in conducting to a successful issue the late war with the Government of Ava, provoked by the unjust aggression of the enemy, prosecuted amid circumstances of very unusual difficulty, and terminated so as to uphold the character of the Company's Government, to maintain the British ascendant in India, and to impress the bordering States with just notions of the national power and resources."'

The Directors and the Court of Proprietors also voted thanks to Lord Amherst 'for his forbearance in not resorting to measures of coercion against the usurper of Bhartpur as long as hopes could reasonably be entertained of accomplishing by means of negotiation the restoration to power of the legitimate Rájá, and for his decision in the failure of negotiation to effect the reduction of that important fortress by force.'

There were only six dissentient voices to the vote of thanks in the Court of Proprietors – consisting of Mr. Hume and his friends. Mr. Hume made every opposition he could devise.

Virtue has triumphed; and the diary returns to

daily life, describes the sights and incidents of life among the Hills, telling of mountains clothed to the summit with cedars and rhododendrons, birds of rare plume, and all the marvels of the Snows.

But there was a land dearer, if not fairer, than the Himálayan Highlands. Lord Amherst had announced his intention of returning to England. On June 15 he and his party quitted Simla. 'We could not but feel sorry to quit this peaceful abode, and the magnificent scenery of those stupendous mountains, but it was our first step towards home.' It is not accurate to say that Lord Amherst 'invented Simla.' Its claims were well understood by officers who served in the North-West, and they had carried its fame to Government House. But he was the first Governor-General who made it a place of retreat from the discomforts of the plains. He set the fashion. Not many years after a lively French traveller described Simla in terms which would not be quite inappropriate to-day. The summer capital of India may thus be said to have been founded by the same Governor-General, who carried British arms beyond the old limits of India; and considering how great has been the effect for evil or for good of the annual exodus to the Hills, the holiday trip was a political event of no small moment.

And now begins the first stage of the homeward way. At Subáthu the Viceregal party are met by bad news. 'The cholera is raging at Náin and hundreds are dying daily. This morning the Rájá, his Ráni, and three hundred attendants came flying through Subáthu on their journey through Náin. Thirty of the latter died; one poor man expired in the bazaar.'

The following quotations give one some idea of what people went through in those days, and with what courage they faced their difficulties :—

'After much deliberation we resolved to proceed this evening on our journey, avoiding as much as possible the sun, living as carefully as possible as to diet, and not sleeping in the infected air. . . . We accordingly set out at 4 o'clock and travelled over high, steep, and almost inaccessible mountains, the sides of which in many places were absolutely perpendicular. The scenery was magnificent, but alas, there were human beings dead and dying scattered on the road, without aid or remedy or a friend to soothe them in their agony or to close their eyes. We proceeded to Bhor, the first stage, and did not arrive till after dark. There being no moon it was perfectly impossible for the bearers to see their way, and it was certainly the most dangerous road that can be imagined. We went to bed much fatigued. . . . We unanimously resolved to return to Subáthu, and started soon after 2 o'clock in the morning, and arrived at 7, shocked and distressed at the wretched scenes of the dead and dying in the fields and roads.

'In the midst of all this Lord Amherst received answers from Mr. Wynn and Sir George Robinson accepting his resignation, but regretting it, and urging him to change his mind.

'On every side come terrible reports. The natives are sacrificing to the gods with music and tomtoms.'

On June 21 they are all at breakfast when one of the suite is taken ill, and by midnight all hope is at an end. 'This sad event has plunged us all into alarm as to our own fate. We have before us a long, fatiguing, and fearful journey, through countries saturated with this dire disease.' This is almost the only complaint the courageous woman makes. One night they rest in the midst of an orange garden with 'fountains innumerable.' They reach Ambála in the early morning; they have no beds; they sleep in their palanquins. As they travel on next day, they have to pass through streams, and lie drenched in cold water. On June 29 they reach Kemaul. 'We had not been in bed since the 24th.' It is not till July 2 that they arrive at Meerut and comparative comfort, thankful to have got over all the difficulties and fatigues as well as they had done. 'Mr. Glyn received us as before in his cool, comfortable and spacious mansion. We were some days and nights recovering from the immense fatigue we had undergone, but did not otherwise suffer. The thermometer ninety and from that to ninety-four.' The officers at Meerut entertained them hospitably; there are compliments and speeches. 'Lord Amherst returns thanks. I never heard Lord Amherst speak more to the feelings or with happier effect. I was thankful when it was over,' his wife writes, 'being overcome with uncontrollable feelings myself.'

Still, the cholera! In one place there were at least 500 men victims to the scourge, and their wives were preparing to ascend the funeral pile, but were all dissuaded, and actually not a single *satí* took place.

We need not follow the itinerary as they measured back the way to Calcutta. One other grief awaited them: for while still travelling they received from Madras the tidings of the death of Sir Thomas Munro —the most trusted of advisers, most faithful of friends. He had intended to return home at the beginning of Lord Amherst's administration; but when the Burmese war was seen to be inevitable, he remained to render all the help his long experience fitted him to give. He fell a victim to the fatal cholera while he was waiting to be relieved of his functions. The yearning for home was never satisfied: it was a pathetic close to a noble life.

One incident by the way deserves mention as an illustration of the temper of a native grandee of the old school. The Nawáb of Murshidábád set out to meet them in state, but on his way received a letter informing him that they would not arrive for a fortnight.

> 'He flew into such a violent rage that it resembled frenzy. He tore off a fine turban with jewels, and threw it into the river. Two rings off his fingers shared the same fate; some valuable filigree work—in short every valuable he could lay his hands on—was thrown overboard. He stamped and raved like a madman, and no one could pacify him. He threatened to cut off his beard and eyebrows, and make a Fakir of himself. Mr. Melville says in his rage he destroyed property to the value of 50,000 rupees—his own to be sure.'

We reach now the record of the last days in India. There is a touching entry of the visit of the sorrowing parents to the burying-ground at Barrackpur, where their son was lying. After remaining a couple of days to recover from their agitation, they proceed to Calcutta, where they are received in great state. Sympathetic farewells and congratulations pour in on every side. A small ship of 500 tons, the *Herald*, is being fitted for their journey home. Good accounts come up from Ava to cheer them—the population has more than doubled—peace, industry, and happiness have taken the place of despotism, extortion, and wretchedness. Sir Charles Metcalfe and other friends vie in attentions and friendly expressions. The new Governor-General is on his way, the new Bishop of Calcutta has landed ; everything seemed prepared for their start when their departure was again delayed by the dangerous illness of their daughter, who lay for many days between life and death : it was not till March 8, 1828 that they are enabled at last to carry their invalid on board. Lord Amherst's departure was in some respects like his reception, the same salutes from Fort William, the same people assembled, 'but,' as she says truly, 'the one was a ceremonial, the other a heartfelt expression of regret.' They are not safe yet. There are risks by sea as well as by land. They encounter tremendous gales of wind, 'appalling tempests.' They prepare for action on one occasion, when an American privateer is seen, and seems to be bearing down upon them. A ball of fire falls from the sky, as large as a 12-pounder, and passes over the mainmast.

On July 21 they pass the Lizard in the night steering for Portsmouth. 'On the 22nd we anchored at Spithead about 8 o'clock, and soon afterwards I had the supreme delight of seeing our three dear sons rush into our cabin—Plymouth, Holmesdale, and Frederick. So unexpected was the delight we were all quite overpowered, and unable to express it but by tears of joy.'

A happy ending to a time chequered with many a sorrow! Lord Amherst was fortunate beyond the common lot; for India has been stern to its English rulers. Thirteen years before, Lord Minto had hastened home grudging every hour of delay that kept him from the wife who was waiting for him in the old Scottish home. He reached England: he left London: but never on this earth was the longed-for meeting to be. 'When, in process of time, it became the part of another generation to "open the places that were closed," and when to those who did so came the desire "to show the image of a voice and make green the flowers that were withered," the last year's letters from Minto to India—so full of hope, of joy—were found tied together with a black string, and inscribed "Poor Fools." With these was a note with an unbroken seal, the last written by Lady Minto to her husband [1].'

Of Lord Amherst's after-life we can speak but briefly. He resumed his place at Court, being Lord

[1] *Lord Minto in India*, edited by his great niece, the Countess of Minto, p. 394.

of the Bedchamber to George IV in 1829–30, and to William IV from 1830–37. In 1834 he was made a Knight Grand Cross of the Hanoverian Order. In 1835 he was appointed Governor-General of Canada, but the Government changing, he never took up the appointment. Suitably enough, the appointment was gazetted on April 1! Having lost his wife in 1837, he married in 1839 the widow of the sixth Earl of Plymouth. In the beautiful park of Montreal he found abundant opportunity of gratifying his taste for trees and flowers, and the many friendships he had formed during his long and varied career gave him the society he loved. His manner was animated: his features, as we see them in the portrait by Sir Thomas Lawrence, were calm, gracious, and regular. 'A statesmanlike face' would be no bad description. He came of a long-lived stock. After his second marriage he spent a good deal of his time at Knole, and there he died on March 13, 1857. In the year of the Mutiny, but, before the tidings of horror came, the veteran passed away, at the ripe age of eighty-four.

INDEX

THE END

RULERS OF INDIA:

THE CLARENDON PRESS SERIES OF INDIAN HISTORICAL RETROSPECTS.

Edited by SIR W. W. HUNTER, K.C.S.I., C.I.E.

Price 2s. 6d. each.

The following volumes have been arranged for up to June, 1894:—

I. *AKBAR: and the Rise of the Mughal Empire*, by COLONEL MALLESON, C.S.I., Author of *A History of the Indian Mutiny; The History of Afghanistan; Herat, &c.* [Published.] Fourth thousand.

II. *ALBUQUERQUE: and the Early Portuguese Settlements in India*, by H. MORSE STEPHENS, Esq., M.A., Balliol College, Lecturer on Indian History at Cambridge, Author of *The French Revolution; The Story of Portugal, &c.* [Published.]

III. *AURANGZÍB: and the Decay of the Mughal Empire*, by STANLEY LANE POOLE, Esq., B.A., Author of *The Coins of the Mughal Emperors; The Life of Stratford Canning; Catalogue of Indian Coins in the British Museum, &c.* [Published.]

IV. *MADHAVA RAO SINDHIA: and the Hindú Reconquest of India*, by H. G. KEENE, Esq., M.A., C.I.E., Author of *The Moghul Empire, &c.* [Published.]

V. *LORD CLIVE: and the Establishment of the English in India*, by COLONEL MALLESON, C.S.I. [Published.]

VI. *DUPLEIX: and the Struggle for India by the European Nations*, by COLONEL MALLESON, C.S.I., Author of *The History of the French in India, &c.* [Published.] Third thousand.

VII. *WARREN HASTINGS: and the Founding of the British Administration*, by CAPTAIN L. J. TROTTER, Author of *India under Victoria, &c.* [Published.] Third thousand.

VIII. *THE MARQUESS CORNWALLIS: and the Consolidation of British Rule*, by W. S. SETON-KARR, Esq., sometime Foreign Secretary to the Government of India, Author of *Selections from the Calcutta Gazettes*, 3 vols. (1784–1805). [Published.] Third thousand.

IX. *HAIDAR ALÍ AND TIPÚ SULTÁN: and the Struggle with the Muhammadan Powers of the South*, by LEWIN BENTHAM BOWRING, Esq., C.S.I., sometime Private Secretary to the Viceroy (Lord Canning) and Chief Commissioner of Mysore. Author of *Eastern Experiences.* [Published.]

X. *THE MARQUESS WELLESLEY: and the Development of the Company into the Supreme Power in India*, by the Rev. W. H. HUTTON, M.A., Fellow and Tutor of St. John's College, Oxford. [Published.]

XI. *THE MARQUESS OF HASTINGS: and the Final Overthrow of the Maráthá Power*, by MAJOR ROSS OF BLADENSBURG, C.B., Coldstream Guards; F.R.G.S. [Published.]

XII. *MOUNTSTUART ELPHINSTONE: and the Making of South-Western India*, by J. S. COTTON, Esq., M.A., formerly Fellow of Queen's College, Oxford, Author of *The Decennial Statement of the Moral and Material Progress and Condition of India*, presented to Parliament (1885), &c. [Published.]

XIII. *SIR THOMAS MUNRO: and the British Settlement of the Madras Presidency*, by JOHN BRADSHAW, Esq., M.A., LL.D., Inspector of Schools, Madras. [Published.]

XIV. *EARL AMHERST: and the British Advance eastwards to Burma*, chiefly from unpublished papers of the Amherst family, by Mrs. ANNE THACKERAY RITCHIE, Author of *Old Kensington, &c.*, assisted by RICHARDSON EVANS, Esq. [Published.]

XV. *LORD WILLIAM BENTINCK: and the Company as a Governing and Non-trading Power*, by DEMETRIUS BOULGER, Esq., Author of *England and Russia in Central Asia; The History of China, &c.* [Published.]

XVI *EARL OF AUCKLAND: and the First Afghan War*, by CAPTAIN L. J. TROTTER, Author of *India under Victoria, &c.* [Published.]

XVII. *VISCOUNT HARDINGE: and the Advance of the British Dominions into the Punjab*, by his Son and Private Secretary, the Right Hon. VISCOUNT HARDINGE. [Published.] Third thousand.

XVIII. *RANJIT SINGH: and the Sikh Barrier between our Growing Empire and Central Asia*, by SIR LEPEL GRIFFIN, K.C.S.I., Author of *The Punjab Chiefs, &c.* [Published.] Third thousand.

XIX. *RUSSELL COLVIN: the last Lieutenant-Governor of the North-Western Provinces under the Company*, by his son SIR AUCKLAND COLVIN, K.C.S.I., late Lieutenant-Governor of the North-Western Provinces. [Shortly.]

XX. *THE MARQUESS OF DALHOUSIE: and the Final Development of the Company's Rule*, by SIR WILLIAM WILSON HUNTER, K.C.S.I., M.A. [Published.] Fifth thousand.

XXI. *CLYDE AND STRATHNAIRN: and the Suppression of the Great Revolt*, by MAJOR-GENERAL SIR OWEN TUDOR BURNE, K.C.S.I., sometime Military Secretary to the Commander-in-Chief in India. [Published.] Third thousand.

XXII. *EARL CANNING: and the Transfer of India from the Company to the Crown*, by SIR HENRY S. CUNNINGHAM, K.C.I.E., M.A., Author of *British India and its Rulers, &c.* [Published.] Third thousand.

XXIII. *LORD LAWRENCE: and the Reconstruction of India under the Crown*, by SIR CHARLES UMPHERSTON AITCHISON, K.C.S.I., LL.D., formerly Foreign Secretary to the Government of India, and late Lieutenant-Governor of the Punjab. [Published.]

XXIV. *THE EARL OF MAYO: and the Consolidation of the Queen's Rule in India*, by SIR WILLIAM WILSON HUNTER, K.C.S.I., M.A., LL.D. [Published.] Third thousand.

SUPPLEMENTARY VOLUMES.

A BRIEF HISTORY OF THE INDIAN PEOPLES, by SIR WILLIAM WILSON HUNTER, K.C.S.I. Twentieth Edition; 78th thousand. Price 3*s.* 6*d.* [Published.]

JAMES THOMASON: and the British Settlement of North-Western India, by SIR RICHARD TEMPLE, Bart., M.P., formerly Lieutenant-Governor of Bengal, and Governor of Bombay. Price 3*s.* 6*d.* [Published.]

Opinions of the Press

ON

SIR WILLIAM HUNTER'S 'DALHOUSIE.'

'An interesting and exceedingly readable volume. . . . . Sir William Hunter has produced a valuable work about an important epoch in English history in India, and he has given us a pleasing insight into the character of a remarkable Englishman. The "Rulers of India" series, which he has initiated, thus makes a successful beginning in his hands with one who ranks among the greatest of the great names which will be associated with the subject.'—*The Times.*

'To no one is the credit for the improved condition of public intelligence [regarding India] more due than to Sir William Hunter. From the beginning of his career as an Indian Civilian he has devoted a rare literary faculty to the task of enlightening his countrymen on the subject of England's greatest dependency. . . . By inspiring a small army of fellow-labourers with his own spirit, by inducing them to conform to his own method, and shaping a huge agglomeration of facts into a lucid and intelligible system, Sir W. Hunter has brought India and its innumerable interests within the pale of achievable knowledge, and has given definite shape to the truths which its history establishes and the problems which it suggests. . . . Such contributions to literature are apt to be taken as a matter of course, because their highest merit is to conceal the labour, and skill, and knowledge involved in their production; but they raise the whole level of public intelligence, and generate an atmosphere in which the baleful influences of folly, ignorance, prejudice, and presumption dwindle and disappear.'—*Saturday Review.*

'Admirably calculated to impart in a concise and agreeable form a clear general outline of the history of our great Indian Empire.'—*Economist.*

'A skilful and most attractive picture. . . . The author has made good use of public and private documents, and has enjoyed the privilege of being aided by the deceased statesman's family. His little work is, consequently, a valuable contribution to modern history.'—*Academy.*

'The book should command a wide circle of readers, not only for its author's sake and that of its subject, but partly at least on account of the very attractive way in which it has been published at the moderate price of half-a-crown. But it is, of course, by its intrinsic merits alone that a work of this nature should be judged. And those merits are everywhere conspicuous. . . . A writer whose thorough mastery of all Indian subjects has been acquired by years of practical experience and patient research.'—*The Athenæum.*

'Never have we been so much impressed by the great literary abilities of Sir William Hunter as we have been by the perusal of "The Marquess of Dalhousie." . . . The knowledge displayed by the writer of the motives of Lord Dalhousie's action, of the inner working of his mind, is so complete, that Lord Dalhousie himself, were he living, could not state them more clearly. . . . Sir William Hunter's style is so clear, his language so vivid, and yet so simple, conveying the impressions he wishes so perspicuously that they cannot but be understood, that the work must have a place in every library, in every home, we might say indeed every cottage.'—*Evening News.*

'Sir William Hunter has written an admirable little volume on "The Marquess of Dalhousie" for his series of the "Rulers of India." It can be read at a sitting, yet its references—expressed or implied—suggest the study and observation of half a life-time.'—*The Daily News.*

Opinions of the Press
ON
SIR WILLIAM HUNTER'S 'LORD MAYO.'

'Sir William W. Hunter has contributed a brief but admirable biography of the Earl of Mayo to the series entitled "Rulers of India," edited by himself (Oxford, at the Clarendon Press).'—*The Times.*

'In telling this story in the monograph before us, Sir William Hunter has combined his well-known literary skill with an earnest sympathy and fulness of knowledge which are worthy of all commendation. . . . The world is indebted to the author for a fit and attractive record of what was eminently a noble life.'—*The Academy.*

'The sketch of The Man is full of interest, drawn as it is with complete sympathy, understanding, and appreciation. But more valuable is the account of his administration. No one can show so well and clearly as Sir William Hunter does what the policy of Lord Mayo contributed to the making of the Indian Empire of to-day.'—*The Scotsman.*

'Sir William Hunter has given us a monograph in which there is a happy combination of the essay and the biography. We are presented with the main features of Lord Mayo's administration unencumbered with tedious details which would interest none but the most official of Anglo-Indians; while in the biography the man is brought before us, not analytically, but in a life-like portrait.'—*Vanity Fair.*

'The story of his life Sir W. W. Hunter tells in well-chosen language—clear, succinct, and manly. Sir W. W. Hunter is in sympathy with his subject, and does full justice to Mayo's strong, genuine nature. Without exaggeration and in a direct, unaffected style, as befits his theme, he brings the man and his work vividly before us.'—*The Glasgow Herald.*

'All the knowledge acquired by personal association, familiarity with administrative details of the Indian Government, and a strong grasp of the vast problems to be dealt with, is utilised in this presentation of Lord Mayo's personality and career. Sir W. Hunter, however, never overloads his pages, and the outlines of the sketch are clear and firm.'—*The Manchester Express.*

'This is another of the "Rulers of India" series, and it will be hard to beat. . . . Sir William Hunter's perception and expression are here at their very best.'—*The Pall Mall Gazette.*

'The latest addition to the "Rulers of India" series yields to none of its predecessors in attractiveness, vigour, and artistic portraiture. . . . The final chapter must either be copied verbally and literally—which the space at our disposal will not permit—or be left to the sorrowful perusal of the reader. The man is not to be envied who can read it with dry eyes.'—*Allen's Indian Mail.*

'The little volume which has just been brought out is a study of Lord Mayo's career by one who knew all about it and was in full sympathy with it. . . . Some of these chapters are full of spirit and fire. The closing passages, the picture of the Viceroy's assassination, cannot fail to make any reader hold his breath. We know what is going to happen, but we are thrilled as if we did not know it, and were still held in suspense. The event itself was so terribly tragic that any ordinary description might seem feeble and laggard. But in this volume we are made to feel as we must have felt if we had been on the spot and seen the murderer "fastened like a tiger" on the back of the Viceroy.'—*Daily News*, Leading Article.

Opinions of the Press

ON

MR. W. S. SETON-KARR'S 'CORNWALLIS.'

'This new volume of the "Rulers of India" series keeps up to the high standard set by the author of "The Marquess of Dalhousie." For dealing with the salient passages in Lord Cornwallis's Indian career no one could have been better qualified than the whilom foreign secretary to Lord Lawrence.'—*The Athenæum.*

'Lord Cornwallis has been very properly included in the list of those "Rulers of India" whose biographies are calculated to illustrate the past growth and present development of the English administration in that country. His name is connected with several great measures, which more, perhaps, than any others have given a special colour to our rule, have influenced the course of subsequent legislation, and have made the Civil Service what it at present is. He completed the administrative fabric of which Warren Hastings, in the midst of unexampled difficulties and vicissitudes, had laid the foundation.'—*The Saturday Review.*

'We hope that the volumes on the "Rulers of India" which are being published by the Clarendon Press are carefully read by a large section of the public. There is a dense wall of ignorance still standing between the average Englishman and the greatest dependency of the Crown; although we can scarcely hope to see it broken down altogether, some of these admirable biographies cannot fail to lower it a little. . . . Mr. Seton-Karr has succeeded in the task, and he has not only presented a large mass of information, but he has brought it together in an attractive form. . . . We strongly recommend the book to all who wish to enlarge the area of their knowledge with reference to India.'—*New York Herald.*

'The "Rulers of India" series. This outcome of the Clarendon Press grows in value as it proceeds. The account of Cornwallis is from the pen of Mr. W. Seton-Karr, who was formerly Foreign Secretary to the Government of India, and whose acquaintance with Eastern affairs has been of obvious service to him in the compilation of this useful manual.'—*The Globe.*

'One might almost say that the history of our great Indian Empire might be read with comparative ease in the excellent "Rulers of India Series," published at the Clarendon Press at Oxford. . . . Of Cornwallis it might be said he transformed the East India Company's servants from merchants to administrators, and determined to place them above jobbery, which he despised.'—*The Independent.*

'We have already expressed our sense of the value and timeliness of the series of Indian historical retrospects now issuing, under the editorship of Sir W. W. Hunter, from the Clarendon Press. It is somewhat less than fair to say of Mr. Seton-Karr's monograph upon Cornwallis that it reaches the high standard of literary workmanship which that series has maintained. . . . His accurate and lucid summary of the necessities which dictated Cornwallis's policy, and the methods by which he initiated and, to a great extent, effected, the transformation of our rule in India from the lines of an Oriental despotism to those with which we are now familiar, is as attractive as it is instructive.'—*The Literary World.*

Opinions of the Press

ON

COLONEL MALLESON'S 'DUPLEIX.'

'In the character of Dupleix there was the element of greatness that contact with India seems to have generated in so many European minds, French as well as English, and a broad capacity for government, which, if suffered to have full play, might have ended in giving the whole of Southern India to France. Even as it was, Colonel Malleson shows how narrowly the prize slipped from French grasp. In 1783 the Treaty of Versailles arrived just in time to save the British power from extinction.'—*Times.*

'One of the best of Sir W. Hunter's interesting and valuable series. Colonel Malleson writes out of the fulness of familiarity, moving with ease over a field which he had long ago surveyed in every nook and corner. To do a small book as well as this on Dupleix has been done, will be recognised by competent judges as no small achievement. When one considers the bulk of the material out of which the little volume has been distilled, one can still better appreciate the labour and dexterity involved in the performance.'—*Academy.*

'A most compact and effective history of the French in India in a little handbook of 180 pages.'—*Nonconformist.*

'Well arranged, lucid and eminently readable, an excellent addition to a most useful series.'—*Record.*

COLONEL MALLESON'S 'AKBAR.'

'Colonel Malleson's interesting monograph on Akbar in the "Rulers of India" (Clarendon Press) should more than satisfy the general reader. Colonel Malleson traces the origin and foundation of the Mughal Empire; and, as an introduction to the history of Muhammadan India, the book leaves nothing to be desired.'—*St. James's Gazette.*

'This volume will, no doubt, be welcomed, even by experts in Indian history, in the light of a new, clear, and terse rendering of an old, but not worn-out theme. It is a worthy and valuable addition to Sir W. Hunter's promising series.'—*Athenæum.*

'Colonel Malleson has broken ground new to the general reader. The story of Akbar is briefly but clearly told, with an account of what he was and what he did, and how he found and how he left India. . . . The native chronicles of the reign are many, and from them it is still possible, as Colonel Malleson has shown, to construct a living portrait of this great and mighty potentate.'—*Scots Observer.*

'The brilliant historian of the Indian Mutiny has been assigned in this volume of the series an important epoch and a strong personality for critical study, and he has admirably fulfilled his task. . . . Alike in dress and style, this volume is a fit companion for its predecessor.'—*Manchester Guardian.*

Opinions of the Press

ON

CAPTAIN TROTTER'S 'WARREN HASTINGS.'

'The publication, recently noticed in this place, of the "Letters, Despatches, and other State Papers preserved in the Foreign Department of the Government of India, 1772–1785," has thrown entirely new light from the most authentic sources on the whole history of Warren Hastings and his government of India. Captain L. J. Trotter's WARREN HASTINGS is accordingly neither inopportune nor devoid of an adequate *raison d'être*. Captain Trotter is well known as a competent and attractive writer on Indian history, and this is not the first time that Warren Hastings has supplied him with a theme.'—*The Times.*

'He has put his best work into this memoir. . . . His work is of distinct literary merit, and is worthy of a theme than which British history presents none nobler. It is a distinct gain to the British race to be enabled, as it now may, to count the great Governor-General among those heroes for whom it need not blush.'—*Scotsman.*

'Captain Trotter has done his work well, and his volume deserves to stand with that on Dalhousie by Sir William Hunter. Higher praise it would be hard to give it.'—*New York Herald.*

'Captain Trotter has done full justice to the fascinating story of the splendid achievements of a great Englishman.'—*Manchester Guardian.*

'A brief but admirable biography of the first Governor-General of India.'—*Newcastle Chronicle.*

'A book which all must peruse who desire to be "up to date" on the subject.'—*The Globe.*

MR. KEENE'S 'MADHAVA RAO SINDHIA.'

'Mr. Keene has the enormous advantage, not enjoyed by every producer of a book, of knowing intimately the topic he has taken up. He has compressed into these 203 pages an immense amount of information, drawn from the best sources, and presented with much neatness and effect.'—*The Globe.*

'Mr. Keene tells the story with knowledge and impartiality, and also with sufficient graphic power to make it thoroughly readable. The recognition of Sindhia in the "Rulers" series is just and graceful, and it cannot fail to give satisfaction to the educated classes of our Indian fellow-subjects.'—*North British Daily Mail.*

'The volume bears incontestable proofs of the expenditure of considerable research by the author, and sustains the reputation he had already acquired by his "Sketch of the History of Hindustan."'—*Freeman's Journal.*

'Among the eighteen rulers of India included in the scheme of Sir William Hunter only five are natives of India, and of these the great Madhoji Sindhia is, with the exception of Akbar, the most illustrious. Mr. H. G. Keene, a well-known and skilful writer on Indian questions, is fortunate in his subject, for the career of the greatest bearer of the historic name of Sindhia covered the exciting period from the capture of Delhi, the Imperial capital, by the Persian Nadir Shah, to the occupation of the same city by Lord Lake. . . . Mr. Keene gives a lucid description of his subsequent policy, especially towards the English when he was brought face to face with Warren Hastings.'—*The Daily Graphic.*

P 2

Opinions of the Press

ON

MAJOR-GENERAL SIR OWEN BURNE'S 'CLYDE AND STRATHNAIRN.'

'In "Clyde and Strathnairn," a contribution to Sir William Hunter's excellent "Rulers of India" series (Oxford, at the Clarendon Press), Sir Owen Burne gives a lucid sketch of the military history of the Indian Mutiny and its suppression by the two great soldiers who give their names to his book. The space is limited for so large a theme, but Sir Owen Burne skilfully adjusts his treatment to his limits, and rarely violates the conditions of proportion imposed upon him.' . . . 'Sir Owen Burne does not confine himself exclusively to the military narrative. He gives a brief sketch of the rise and progress of the Mutiny, and devotes a chapter to the Reconstruction which followed its suppression.' . . . '—well written, well proportioned, and eminently worthy of the series to which it belongs.'—*The Times.*

'Sir Owen Burne who, by association, experience, and relations with one of these generals, is well qualified for the task, writes with knowledge, perspicuity, and fairness.'—*Saturday Review.*

'As a brief record of a momentous epoch in India this little book is a remarkable piece of clear, concise, and interesting writing.'—*The Colonies and India.*

'Sir Owen Burne has written this book carefully, brightly, and with excellent judgment, and we in India cannot read such a book without feeling that he has powerfully aided the accomplished editor of the series in a truly patriotic enterprise.'—*Bombay Gazette.*

'The volume on "Clyde and Strathnairn" has just appeared and proves to be a really valuable addition to the series. Considering its size and the extent of ground it covers it is one of the best books about the Indian Mutiny of which we know.'—*Englishman.*

'Sir Owen Burne, who has written the latest volume for Sir William Hunter's "Rulers of India" series, is better qualified than any living person to narrate, from a military standpoint, the story of the suppression of the Indian Mutiny.'—*Daily Telegraph.*

'Sir Owen Burne's book on "Clyde and Strathnairn" is worthy to rank with the best in the admirable series to which it belongs.'—*Manchester Examiner.*

'The book is admirably written; and there is probably no better sketch, equally brief, of the stirring events with which it deals.' *Scotsman.*

'Sir Owen Burne, from the part he played in the Indian Mutiny, and from his long connexion with the Government of India, and from the fact that he was military secretary of Lord Strathnairn both in India and in Ireland, is well qualified for the task which he has undertaken.'—*The Athenæum.*

Opinions of the Press

ON

VISCOUNT HARDINGE'S 'LORD HARDINGE.'

'An exception to the rule that biographies ought not to be entrusted to near relatives. Lord Hardinge, a scholar and an artist, has given us an accurate record of his father's long and distinguished services. There is no filial exaggeration. The author has dealt with some controversial matters with skill, and has managed to combine truth with tact and regard for the feelings of others.'—*The Saturday Review.*

'This interesting life reveals the first Lord Hardinge as a brave, just, able man, the very soul of honour, admired and trusted equally by friends and political opponents. The biographer . . . has produced a most engaging volume, which is enriched by many private and official documents that have not before seen the light.'—*The Anti-Jacobin.*

'Lord Hardinge has accomplished a grateful, no doubt, but, from the abundance of material and delicacy of certain matters, a very difficult task in a workmanlike manner, marked by restraint and lucidity.'—*The Pall Mall Gazette.*

'His son and biographer has done his work with a true appreciation of proportion, and has added substantially to our knowledge of the Sutlej Campaign.'—*Vanity Fair.*

'The present Lord Hardinge is in some respects exceptionally well qualified to tell the tale of the eventful four years of his father's Governor-Generalship.'—*The Times.*

'It contains a full account of everything of importance in Lord Hardinge's military and political career; it is arranged . . . so as to bring into special prominence his government of India; and it gives a lifelike and striking picture of the man.'—*Academy.*

'The style is clear, the treatment dispassionate, and the total result a manual which does credit to the interesting series in which it figures.' —*The Globe.*

'The concise and vivid account which the son has given of his father's career will interest many readers.'—*The Morning Post.*

'Eminently readable for everybody. The history is given succinctly, and the unpublished letters quoted are of real value.'—*The Colonies and India.*

'Compiled from public documents, family papers, and letters, this brief biography gives the reader a clear idea of what Hardinge was, both as a soldier and as an administrator.'—*The Manchester Examiner.*

'An admirable sketch.'—*The New York Herald.*

'The Memoir is well and concisely written, and is accompanied by an excellent likeness after the portrait by Sir Francis Grant.'—*The Queen.*

Opinions of the Press
ON
SIR HENRY CUNNINGHAM'S 'EARL CANNING.'

'Sir Henry Cunningham's rare literary skill and his knowledge of Indian life and affairs are not now displayed for the first time, and he has enjoyed exceptional advantages in dealing with his present subject. Lord Granville, Canning's contemporary at school and colleague in public life and one of his oldest friends, furnished his biographer with notes of his recollections of the early life of his friend. Sir Henry Cunningham has also been allowed access to the Diary of Canning's private secretary, to the Journal of his military secretary, and to an interesting correspondence between the Governor-General and his great lieutenant, Lord Lawrence.'—*The Times.*

'Sir H. S. Cunningham has succeeded in writing the history of a critical period in so fair and dispassionate a manner as to make it almost a matter of astonishment that the motives which he has so clearly grasped should ever have been misinterpreted, and the results which he indicates so grossly misjudged. Nor is the excellence of his work less conspicuous from the literary than from the political and historical point of view.'—*Glasgow Herald.*

'Sir H. S. Cunningham has treated his subject adequately. In vivid language he paints his word-pictures, and with calm judicial analysis he also proves himself an able critic of the actualities, causes, and results of the outbreak, also a temperate, just appreciator of the character and policy of Earl Canning.'—*The Court Journal.*

REV. W. H. HUTTON'S 'MARQUESS WELLESLEY.'

'Mr. Hutton has brought to his task an open mind, a trained historical judgement, and a diligent study of a great body of original material. Hence he is enabled to present a true, authentic, and original portrait of one of the greatest of Anglo-Indian statesmen, doing full justice to his military policy and achievements, and also to his statesmanlike efforts for the organization and consolidation of that Empire which he did so much to sustain.'—*Times.*

'To the admirable candour and discrimination which characterize Mr. Hutton's monograph as an historical study must be added the literary qualities which distinguish it and make it one of the most readable volumes of the series. The style is vigorous and picturesque, and the arrangement of details artistic in its just regard for proportion and perspective. In short, there is no point of view from which the work deserves anything but praise.'—*Glasgow Herald.*

'The Rev. W. H. Hutton has done his work well, and achieves with force and lucidity the task he sets himself: to show how, under Wellesley, the Indian company developed and ultimately became the supreme power in India. To our thinking his estimate of this great statesman is most just.'—*Black and White.*

'Mr. Hutton has told the story of Lord Wellesley's life in an admirable manner, and has provided a most readable book.'—*Manchester Examiner.*

'Mr. Hutton's range of information is wide, his division of subjects appropriate, and his diction scholarly and precise.'—*Saturday Review.*

Opinions of the Press

ON

MR. DEMETRIUS BOULGER'S 'LORD WILLIAM BENTINCK.'

'The "Rulers of India" series has received a valuable addition in the biography of the late Lord William Bentinck. The subject of this interesting memoir was a soldier as well as a statesman. He was mainly instrumental in bringing about the adoption of the overland route and in convincing the people of India that a main factor in English policy was a disinterested desire for their welfare. Lord William's despatches and minutes, several of which are textually reproduced in Mr. Boulger's praiseworthy little book, display considerable literary skill and are one and all State papers of signal worth.'—*Daily Telegraph.*

'Mr. Boulger is no novice in dealing with Oriental history and Oriental affairs, and in the career of Lord William Bentinck he has found a theme very much to his taste, which he treats with adequate knowledge and literary skill.'—*The Times.*

'His frontier policy was conciliatory, but full of foresight. His minute on the subject of Afghanistan and the advance of Russia in Asia may be read with advantage to-day, nearly sixty years after it was written. Similarly, his observations on the armies of India have lost by no means all of their force, and Mr. Boulger has done a public service in printing the document.'—*Daily News.*

'How all this was effected has been clearly and forcibly set forth by Mr. Boulger. Though concisely written, his memoir omits nothing really essential to a thorough understanding and just appreciation of Bentinck's work, and of the results which flowed from it, even after he had ceased to be at the head of Indian affairs. Mr. Boulger's estimate of the statesman is eminently fair and dispassionate, based on a thorough knowledge of his administration in all its details. Altogether the little work is a valuable addition to a most useful series.'—*Glasgow Herald.*

'Mr. Boulger writes clearly and well, and his volume finds an accepted place in the very useful and informing series which Sir William Wilson Hunter is editing so ably.'—*Independent.*

'Lord William Bentinck occupies a distinct place among Indian Governors-General. His rule may be regarded as the commencement of an epoch. Mr. Boulger has not to tell a stirring story of war and conquest, but the record of Lord William Bentinck's domestic reforms, by which he began the regeneration of India, is as deeply interesting and certainly as well worth studying as any chapter of preceding Indian history. Mr. Boulger has produced an excellent brief history of the period, and a capital life of the Governor-General. The volume is one of the series of "Rulers of India," and none of them is better worthy of perusal.'—*The Scotsman.*

'Mr. Boulger, it should be added, has done his work with care and judgement.'—*The Globe.*

Opinions of the Press

ON

SIR LEPEL GRIFFIN'S 'RANJIT SINGH.'

'Sir Lepel Griffin treats his topic with thorough mastery, and his account of the famous Mahárájá and his times is, consequently, one of the most valuable as well as interesting volumes of the series of which it forms a part.'—*The Globe.*

'We can thoroughly praise Sir Lepel Griffin's work as an accurate and appreciative account of the beginnings and growth of the Sikh religion and of the temporal power founded upon it by a strong and remorseless chieftain.'—*The Times.*

'One of the best books recently published on any Indian question.'—*The Manchester Guardian.*

'The reading public has here the essence of all that is worth knowing about the period.'—*The Glasgow Evening News.*

'From first to last it is a model of what such a work should be, and a classic. The book is one of the most interesting historical sketches ever given to the public, and illustrated throughout by a unique acquaintance with the subject, and exquisite point.'—*The St. Stephen's Review.*

'Sir Lepel has done justice to one of the most interesting and picturesque episodes of Indian history. In every respect, but perhaps most of all from the point of view of the general reader who does not wholly subordinate enjoyment to instruction, the volume is a most acceptable addition to the series.'—*The Glasgow Herald.*

'The monograph could not have been entrusted to more capable hands than those of Sir Lepel Griffin, who spent his official life in the Punjaub, and is an expert in all the knowledge appertaining to a thorough acquaintance, practical and bookish, with that province. This is an excellent sketch of Ranjit Singh, his people, and his short-lived kingdom.'—*The Scotsman.*

'At once the shortest and best history of the rise and fall of the Sikh monarchy.'—*The North British Daily Mail.*

'An excellent piece of work—candid, discriminating, and well-balanced.'—*The Yorkshire Post.*

'Not only a biography of the Napoleon of the East, but a luminous picture of his country; the chapter on Sikh Theocracy being a notable example of compact thought. For grasp of subject, careful treatment, and charm of narration, this volume is second to none in the series. It may fairly be said to "speak volumes," and possesses an exceptional value as being by our chief authority on Punjab matters.'—*The Liverpool Mercury.*

'The career of no Indian ruler since the Moghul Aurungzebe and the Mahratta Sivaji presents a finer subject for the historian; and it would be difficult to find a writer better qualified than Sir Lepel Griffin to deal with such a subject.'—*The St. James's Gazette.*

'A truly masterly account of Ranjit Singh and the short-lived Sikh monarchy of Lahore.'—*The World.*

'The sketch is in every respect a masterly one, and proves its author to be capable of producing something on a larger scale that would be unsurpassed among histories of our great dependency.'—*The Literary World.*

Opinions of the Press

ON

MR. J. S. COTTON'S 'MOUNTSTUART ELPHINSTONE.'

'Sir William Hunter, the editor of the series to which this book belongs, was happily inspired when he entrusted the Life of Elphinstone, one of the most scholarly of Indian rulers, to Mr. Cotton, who, himself a scholar of merit and repute, is brought by the nature of his daily avocations into close and constant relations with scholars. . . . We live in an age in which none but specialists can afford to give more time to the memoirs of even the most distinguished Anglo-Indians than will be occupied by reading Mr. Cotton's two hundred pages. He has performed his task with great skill and good sense. This is just the kind of Life of himself which the wise, kindly, high-souled man, who is the subject of it, would read with pleasure in the Elysian Fields.'—Sir M. E. Grant Duff, in *The Academy*.

'To so inspiring a theme few writers are better qualified to do ample justice than the author of "The Decennial Statement of the Moral and Material Progress and Condition of India." Sir T. Colebrooke's larger biography of Elphinstone appeals mainly to Indian specialists, but Mr. Cotton's slighter sketch is admirably adapted to satisfy the growing demand for a knowledge of Indian history and of the personalities of Anglo-Indian statesmen which Sir William Hunter has done so much to create.'—*The Times*.

DR. BRADSHAW'S 'SIR THOMAS MUNRO.'

'A most valuable, compact and interesting memoir for those looking forward to or engaged in the work of Indian administration.'—*Scotsman*.

'It is a careful and sympathetic survey of a life which should always serve as an example to the Indian soldier and civilian.'—*Yorkshire Post*.

'A true and vivid record of Munro's life-work in almost autobiographical form.'—*Glasgow Herald*.

'Of the work before us we have nothing but praise. The story of Munro's career in India is in itself of exceptional interest and importance.'—*Freeman's Journal*.

'The work could not have been better done; it is a monument of pains-taking care, exhaustive research, and nice discrimination.'—*People*.

'This excellent and spirited little monograph catches the salient points of Munro's career, and supplies some most valuable quotations from his writings and papers.'—*Manchester Guardian*.

'It would be impossible to imagine a more attractive and at the same time instructive book about India.'—*Liverpool Courier*.

'It is one of the best volumes of this excellent series.'—*Imperial and Asiatic Quarterly Review*.

'The book throughout is arranged in an admirably clear manner and there is evident on every page a desire for truth, and nothing but the truth.'—*Commerce*.

'A clear and scholarly piece of work.'—*Indian Journal of Education*.

Opinions of the Press

ON

MR. MORSE STEPHENS' 'ALBUQUERQUE.'

'Mr. Stephens' able and instructive monograph . . . We may commend Mr. Morse Stephens' volume, both as an adequate summary of an important period in the history of the relations between Asia and Europe, and as a suggestive treatment of the problem of why Portugal failed and England succeeded in founding an Indian Empire.'—*The Times.*

'Mr. H. Morse Stephens has made a very readable book out of the foundation of the Portuguese power in India. According to the practice of the series to which it belongs it is called a life of Affonso de Albuquerque, but the Governor is only the central and most important figure in a brief history of the Portuguese in the East down to the time when the Dutch and English intruded on their preserves . . . A pleasantly-written and trustworthy book on an interesting man and time.' —*The Saturday Review.*

'Mr. Morse Stephens' *Albuquerque* is a solid piece of work, well put together, and full of interest.'—*The Athenæum.*

'Mr. Morse Stephens' studies in Indian and Portuguese history have thoroughly well qualified him for approaching the subject . . . He has presented the facts of Albuquerque's career, and sketched the events marking the rule of his predecessor Almeida, and of his immediate successors in the Governorship and Viceroyalty of India in a compact, lucid, and deeply interesting form.'—*The Scotsman.*

SIR CHARLES AITCHISON'S 'LORD LAWRENCE.'

'No man knows the policy, principles, and character of John Lawrence better than Sir Charles Aitchison. The salient features and vital principles of his work as a ruler, first in the Punjab, and afterwards as Viceroy, are set forth with remarkable clearness.'—*Scotsman.*

'A most admirable sketch of the great work done by Sir John Lawrence, who not only ruled India, but saved it.'—*Manchester Examiner.*

'Sir Charles Aitchison's narrative is uniformly marked by directness, order, clearness, and grasp; it throws additional light into certain nooks of Indian affairs; and it leaves upon the mind a very vivid and complete impression of Lord Lawrence's vigorous, resourceful, discerning, and valiant personality.'—*Newcastle Daily Chronicle.*

'Sir Charles knows the Punjab thoroughly, and has made this little book all the more interesting by his account of the Punjab under John Lawrence and his subordinates.'—*Yorkshire Post.*

Opinions of the Press

ON

LEWIN BENTHAM BOWRING'S 'HAIDAR ALÍ AND TIPÚ SULTÁN.'

'Mr. Bowring's portraits are just, and his narrative of the continuous military operations of the period full and accurate.'—*Times.*

'The story has been often written, but never better or more concisely than here, where the father and son are depicted vividly and truthfully "in their habit as they lived." There is not a volume of the whole series which is better done than this, or one which shows greater insight.'—*Daily Chronicle.*

'Mr. Bowring has been well chosen to write this memorable history, because he has had the best means of collecting it, having himself formerly been Chief Commissioner of Mysore. The account of the Mysore war is well done, and Mr. Bowring draws a stirring picture of our determined adversary.'—*Army and Navy Gazette.*

'An excellent example of compression and precision. Many volumes might be written about the long war in Mysore, and we cannot but admire the skill with which Mr. Bowring has condensed the history of the struggle. His book is as terse and concise as a book can be.'—*North British Daily Mail.*

'Mr. Bowring's book is one of the freshest and best of a series most valuable to all interested in the concerns of the British Empire in the East.'—*English Mail.*

'The story of the final capture of Seringapatam is told with skill and graphic power by Mr. Bowring, who throughout the whole work shows himself a most accurate and interesting historian.'—*Perthshire Advertiser.*

COLONEL MALLESON'S 'LORD CLIVE.'

'This book gives a spirited and accurate sketch of a very extraordinary personality.'—*Speaker.*

'Colonel Malleson writes a most interesting account of Clive's great work in India—so interesting that, having begun to read it, one is unwilling to lay it aside until the last page has been reached. The character of Clive as a leader of men, and especially as a cool, intrepid, and resourceful general, is ably described; and at the same time the author never fails to indicate the far-reaching political schemes which inspired the valour of Clive and laid the foundation of our Indian Empire.'—*North British Daily Mail.*

'This monograph is admirably written by one thoroughly acquainted and in love with his subject.'—*Glasgow Herald.*

'No one is better suited than Colonel Malleson to write on Clive, and he has performed his task with distinct success. The whole narrative is, like everything Colonel Malleson writes, clear and full of vigour.'—*Yorkshire Post.*

'Colonel Malleson is reliable and fair, and the especial merit of his book is that it always presents a clear view of the whole of the vast theatre in which Clive gradually produces such an extraordinary change of scene.'—*Newcastle Daily Chronicle.*

Opinions of the Press

ON

CAPT. TROTTER'S 'EARL OF AUCKLAND.'

'A vivid account of the causes, conduct, and consequences of "the costly, fruitless, and unrighteous" Afghan War of 1838.'—*St. James's Gazette.*

'To write such a monograph was a thankless task, but it has been accomplished with entire success by Captain L. J. Trotter. He has dealt calmly and clearly with Lord Auckland's policy, domestic and military, with its financial results, and with the general tendency of Lord Auckland's rule.'—*Yorkshire Post.*

'To this distressing story (of the First Afghan War) Captain Trotter devotes the major portion of his pages. He tells it well and forcibly; but is drawn, perhaps unavoidably, into the discussion of many topics of controversy which, to some readers, may seem to be hardly as yet finally decided. . . . It is only fair to add that two chapters are devoted to "Lord Auckland's Domestic Policy," and to his relations with "The Native States of India".'—*The Times.*

'Captain Trotter's *Earl of Auckland* is a most interesting book, and its excellence as a condensed, yet luminous, history of the first Afghan War deserves warm recognition.'—*Scotsman.*

'It points a moral which our Indian Rulers cannot afford to forget so long as they still have Russia and Afghanistan to count with.'—*Glasgow Herald.*

Supplementary Volume: price 3s. 6d.

'JAMES THOMASON,' BY SIR RICHARD TEMPLE.

'Sir R. Temple's book possesses a high value as a dutiful and interesting memorial of a man of lofty ideals, whose exploits were none the less memorable because achieved exclusively in the field of peaceful administration.'—*Times.*

'It is the peculiar distinction of this work that it interests a reader less in the official than in the man himself.'—*Scotsman.*

'This is a most interesting book: to those who know India, and knew the man, it is of unparalleled interest, but no one who has the Imperial instinct which has taught the English to rule subject races "for their own welfare" can fail to be struck by the simple greatness of this character.'—*Pall Mall Gazette.*

'Mr. Thomason was a great Indian statesman. He systematized the revenue system of the North-West Provinces, and improved every branch of the administration. He was remarkable, like many great Indians, for the earnestness of his religious faith, and Sir Richard Temple brings this out in an admirable manner.'—*British Weekly.*

'The book is "a portrait drawn by the hand of affection," of one whose life was "a pattern of how a Christian man ought to live." Special prominence is given to the religious aspects of Mr. Thomason's character, and the result is a very readable biographical sketch.'—*Christian.*

Opinions of the Press

ON

MAJOR ROSS OF BLADENSBURG'S 'MARQUESS OF HASTINGS.'

'Major Ross of Bladensburg treats his subject skilfully and attractively, and his biography of Lord Hastings worthily sustains the high reputation of the Series in which it appears.'—*The Times.*

'This monograph is entitled to rank with the best of the Series, the compiler having dealt capably and even brilliantly with his materials.' —*English Mail.*

'Instinct with interest.'—*Glasgow Evening News.*

'As readable as it is instructive.'—*Globe.*

'A truly admirable monograph.'—*Glasgow Herald.*

'Major Ross has done his work admirably, and bids fair to be one of the best writers the Army of our day has given to the country. . . . A most acceptable and entrancing little volume.'—*Daily Chronicle.*

'It is a volume that merits the highest praise. Major Ross of Bladensburg has represented Lord Hastings and his work in India in the right light, faithfully described the country as it was, and in a masterly manner makes one realize how important was the period covered by this volume.'—*Manchester Courier.*

'This excellent monograph ought not to be overlooked by any one who would fully learn the history of British rule in India.'—*Manchester Examiner.*

MR. S. LANE-POOLE'S 'AURANGZÍB.'

'There is no period in Eastern history so full of sensation as the reign of Aurangzíb. . . . Mr. Lane-Poole tells this story admirably; indeed, it were difficult to imagine it better told.'—*National Observer.*

'Mr. Lane-Poole writes learnedly, lucidly, and vigorously. . . . He draws an extremely vivid picture of Aurangzíb, his strange ascetic character, his intrepid courage, his remorseless overthrow of his kinsmen, his brilliant court, and his disastrous policy; and he describes the gradual decline of the Mogul power from Akbar to Aurangzíb with genuine historical insight.'—*Times.*

'A well-knit and capable sketch of one of the most remarkable, perhaps the most interesting, of the Mogul Emperors.'—*Saturday Review.*

'As a study of the man himself, Mr. Lane-Poole's work is marked by a vigour and originality of thought which give it a very exceptional value among works on the subject.'—*Glasgow Herald.*

'The most popular and most picturesque account that has yet appeared . . . a picture of much clearness and force.'—*Globe.*

'A notable sketch, at once scholarly and interesting.'—*English Mail.*

'No one is better qualified than Mr. Stanley Lane-Poole to take up the history and to depict the character of the last of the great Mogul monarchs. . . . Aurangzíb's career is ever a fascinating study.'—*Home News.*

'The author gives a description of the famous city of Sháh Jahán, its palaces, and the ceremonies and pageants of which they were the scene. . . . Mr. Lane-Poole's well-written monograph presents all the most distinctive features of Aurangzíb's character and career.'—*Morning Post.*